The Fun Spanish

A Beginning Spanish Workbook

Level 1

Following the Principles of Charlotte Mason
Learning Spanish One Phrase at a time

Kimberly D. Garcia

Also by Kimberly D. Garcia

The Write from History Series
(A history based classical writing program for students in grades 1 through 5, covering the four year history cycle. Available in both manuscript and cursive.)

The Westminster Shorter Catechism Copybook
(Available in traditional, modern, vertical, and italic cursive.)

Acknowledgements

Thank you to my dear husband
and my wonderful father-in-law.

Introduction

The Fun Spanish is designed for the student that can read and write comfortably in English. It uses everyday vocabulary that is common in a child's life. To get the most from *The Fun Spanish* or any Spanish curriculum, students need exposure to Spanish via many avenues. I recommend Spanish audio tapes with songs and poems, spanish picture books, and time with a native speaker. If the student doesn't have access to a Spanish speaking tutor, an auditory program such as The Learnables or Puertas Abiertas would be very helpful.

The Fun Spanish has been patterned after the principles taught by Ms. Charlotte Mason. She believed that the best way to learn a foreign language was one phrase at a time, introducing five or six new words every day, thereby learning the target language as one learns the primary language. *The Fun Spanish* does similar in a way that I think children will find fun and delightful.

In trying to teach my own children Spanish, I noticed that although we were trying many programs and learning lots of vocabulary, my children were not understanding the Spanish language. As we continued our studies through various programs, I happened to notice that the sillier the Spanish sentences were the more likely my children were to repeat them over the course of the day and the more likely they were to understand them. I took this idea and incorporated it into *The Fun Spanish*.

The Fun Spanish introduces an average of five new words daily in the context of a "fun" sentence that is to be copied, illustrated, and memorized. To understand the sentence, the students must use the vocabulary section on the left page to translate the sentence. While the right page is for copying the Spanish sentence and drawing the picture, the left side contains verb conjugation copywork and a translation exercise. All of the verb copywork is in the present indicative tense; however, the present progressive tense is introduced throughout. This is the English equivalent of the -ing form of the verb.

It is extremely important that students complete all of the copywork and the illustrations. The copywork reinforces vocabulary, while the illustrations help with recall of the fun sentences. Because the sentences are so unusual, the illustrations are crucial.

I have purposely built in repetition of some of the words that are more commonly used such as "querer-to want" and "tener-to have". I have also repeated the use of those words that are more commonly confused by individuals learning Spanish, for example ser and estar which both mean "to be". Ser is a state of being or essence. Estar is a state of temporary condition.

In the text, you will find that *él* and *tú* are accented. This is not the case in all Spanish programs. Because Spanish is a living language, grammatical rules are not consistent across all cultures. And since most beginning children's readers have the *él* and *tú* accented, they are accented here as well.

Schedule for a One Semester Curriculum

Spend the first week reviewing the pronunciation review page and the grammar review page. Refer back to these at any time. For each week thereafter, follow the guidelines below.

For Each Lesson

Day 1

1. Review and memorize the verb in I. Verb Conjugation
2. Copy the underlined words
3. Review vocabulary in II. Vocabulary
4. Skip to Model 1 on the next page and read the fun Spanish sentence
5. Translate the sentence
6. Copy and memorize the day's Spanish sentence
7. Complete the illustration
8. Orally translate the sentence in III. Translation Practice

Day 2

1. Review and memorize the Spanish sentence from Day 1
2. Complete steps 1-8 from day 1 for Model 2

Day 3

1. Review and memorize the Spanish sentences from Days 1 and 2
2. Complete steps 1-8 from day 1 for Model 3

Day 4

1. Review and memorize the Spanish sentences from Days 1, 2, and 3
2. Complete steps 1-8 from day 1 for Model 4

Day 5

1. Complete the Verb Conjugation Review
2. Complete the Vocabulary Review
3. Read the fun Spanish sentences on the next page, numbers 1 through 4
4. Translate one or more of the fun Spanish sentences into English
5. Review the fun sentences for all lessons to date.

Suggested Schedule for a Year Long Curriculum

Spend two weeks per lesson, rather than one. To accomplish this, add a day of review between each model Spanish sentence to be studied, translated, and memorized. This allows for more memorization time.

Answer Key

- At the end of each lesson, translation solutions are included.
- Refer to the pronunciation or the grammar review section whenever needed.

Memorization Suggestions

- At least once per week, review ALL sentences learned to date.

- If your student cannot recall a sentence, let him see the illustration or say the sentence in English and have him translate it into Spanish.

- If the pace of the material is frustrating for your student, stretch the material over two weeks. He may do half of the illustrations one week and finish the second. Or you may opt to have him complete all illustrations on the first week and cover the day five review material, as well as a complete review of all sentences learned to date, on the second week.

- Feel free to change, adjust, or completely modify the schedule to best fit your student's needs.

Good luck and have fun with *The Fun Spanish*.

Pronunciation Review

Letter	Sound	Example
a	ah (father)	c**a**sa
e	ay (say)	f**e**liz
i	ee (feet)	am**i**go
o	oh (so)	n**o**vela
u	oo (smooth)	hasta l**ue**go
c	s (ce, ci)	**c**ena
c	k (all others)	**c**omo
g	h (ge, gi)	**g**eneral
g	g (all others)	**g**ato
h	silent	**h**asta lavista
ll	y (yes)	**ll**amo
q	k (key)	**q**ue
rr	r (roll the r's)	co**rr**er
y	ee(feet)	mu**y**

There are many sites available that will allow you to hear the sound of the alphabet as well as common vocabulary at no charge. To find these websites, search on "Spanish pronunciation guide".

Grammar Review

If your student is not become familiar with these concepts, it will be helpful to cover this material before beginning the program. Review this material as often as necessary.

Nouns

- every noun has gender and number
- masculine nouns usually end with **-o**
  el libro
- feminine nouns usually end with **-a**
  la casa
- some irregular nouns
  la mano is feminine, el mapa is masculine

Articles

Use of **definite articles** which correspond to the English **"the"**

Many nouns follow the example in the table below:

singular masculine	**el** oso	the boy bear
plural masculine	**los** osos	the bears
		(boys or boys and girls)
singular feminine	**la** osa	the girl bear
plural feminine	**las** osas	the girl bears

However, not all nouns follow the pattern:

singular masculine	**la** rata	the boy rat
plural masculine	**las** ratas	the boy rats
singular feminine	**la** rata	the girl rat
plural feminne	**las** ratas	the girl rats

Use of **indefinite articles** which correspond with **"a"**, **"an"**, and **"some"**.

singular masculine	**un** oso	a boy bear
plural masculine	**unos** osos	some bears
		male or (male & female)
singular feminine	**una** osa	a girl bear
plural feminine	**unas** osas	some girl bears

Verbs

- Verb tense used in this book is **Present Indicative** (action occuring)
- three types of verb endings

-ar	habl**ar**
-er	corr**er**
-ir	viv**ir**

- to form the progressive tense (is running) for infinitives with -ar, drop the ar and add -ando and use the correct form of estar.

play (jugar)	I am (estoy)	I am playing. (Yo estoy jugando.)
sing (cantar)	he is (está)	He is singing. (Él está cantando.)

- for infinitives with -er and -ir, drop the er or ir and add -iendo.

eat (comer)	she is (ella está)	She is eating. (Ella está comiendo.)
vivir (live)	you are (tú estás)	You are living. (Tú estás viviendo.)

- the subject pronoun is often omitted in Spanish, however I have included them for this beginning level book

Subject Pronouns

I	yo
You (informal)	tú
He/She	él/ella//Usted
We	nosotros/nosotras
You (all)	vosotros/vosotras
They	Ustedes/ellos/ellas

- Usted, abbreviated Ud., is the formal you. Ustedes, abbreviated Uds., is the plural you.
- From here on the masculine and feminine are abbreviated as follows:
  nosotros/nosotras   nosotros/(as)
- Although the vosotros form of you is used mostly in Spain, I have included in the verb conjugation copywork for familiarization.

Adjectives

- adjectives typically follow the noun

el gato flaco	**the skinny cat**
el oso verde	**the green bear**

- agree in gender and number with a noun

los perros azules	**the blue dogs**
las osas rosadas	**the pink bears**

LESSON 1

I. Verb Conjugation

Read, memorize, and copy the underlined words on the lines provided.

ser (to be)

I am	yo **soy**	_____
You are	tú <u>eres</u>	_____
He/She is	él/ella/Ud. <u>es</u>	_____
We are	nosotros/(as) <u>somos</u>	_____
You (all)	vosotros/(as) <u>sois</u>	_____
They are	Uds./ellos/ellas <u>son</u>	_____

II. Vocabulary

yo.... .I

un gato... .a cat

y... . .and

con... ...with

largas... ..long

soy... ..I am

grande... ..big

verde... ...green

(las) piernas... ..legs

III. Translation Practice

Read the sentence below and repeat in Spanish. Use the vocabulary above for help.

I am a cat.

Model 1 Copy the Spanish sentence(s). Draw a picture.
Lesson 1
Yo soy un gato grande y verde con piernas largas.

_____

_____

I. Verb Conjugation

Read, memorize, and copy the underlined words on the lines provided.

ser (to be)

English	Spanish	
I am	*yo* <u>soy</u>	_____
You are	*tú* <u>eres</u>	_____
He/She is	*él/ella/Ud.* <u>es</u>	_____
We are	*nosotros/(as)* <u>somos</u>	_____
You (all)	*vosotros/(as)* <u>sois</u>	_____
They are	*Uds./ellos/ellas* <u>son</u>	_____

II. Vocabulary

él.....he

una rata......a rat

con......with

(los) pelos......hairs

es......is

naranja......orange

ocho......eight

III. Translation Practice

Read the sentence below and repeat in Spanish. Use the vocabulary above for help.

He is a rat.

Model 2 Copy the Spanish sentence(s). Draw a picture.

Lesson 1

Él es una rata naranja con ocho pelos.

_____

_____

I. Verb Conjugation

Read, memorize, and copy the underlined words on the lines provided.

ser (to be)

I am	yo **soy**	_____
You are	tú <u>eres</u>	_____
He/She is	él/ella/Ud. <u>es</u>	_____
We are	nosotros/(as) <u>somos</u>	_____
You (all)	vosotros/(as) <u>sois</u>	_____
They are	Uds./ellos/ellas <u>son</u>	_____

II. Vocabulary

ella......she

una osa......a bear

con......with

(las) orejas......ears

es......is

rosada......pink

tres......three

III. Translation Practice

Read the sentence below and repeat in Spanish. Use the vocabulary above for help.

She is a bear.

Model 3 Copy the Spanish sentence(s). Draw a picture.
Lesson 1
Ella es una osa rosada con tres orejas.

_____

_____

I. Verb Conjugation

Read, memorize, and copy the underlined words on the lines provided.

ser (to be)

I am	*yo* <u>soy</u>	_____
You are	*tú* <u>eres</u>	_____
He/She is	*él/ella/Ud.* <u>es</u>	_____
We are	*nosotros/(as)* <u>somos</u>	_____
You (all)	*vosotros/(as)* <u>sois</u>	_____
They are	*Uds./ellos/ellas* <u>son</u>	_____

II. Vocabulary

nosotros.......we   somos......we are (state of being)

(los) amigos......friends   estamos......we are (temporary condition)

jugando.....playing   en......in

el jardín......the garden   (jugar......play)

III. Translation Practice

Read the sentence below and repeat in Spanish. Use the vocabulary above for help.

We are in the garden.

8

Model 4 Copy the Spanish sentence(s). Draw a picture.
Lesson 1
Nosotros somos amigos. Nosotros estamos
jugando en el jardín.

Verb Conjugation Review

Write the conjugation of the verb _ser_. Use the previous page for help, if needed.

yo _____   nosotros/(as) _____

tú _____   vosotros/(as) _____

él/ella/Ud. _____   Uds./ellos/ellas _____

Vocabulary Review

Translate the following words. Remember to add the appropriate article, _el_, _la_, _los_, or _las_. Use the vocabulary from the previous pages for help, if needed.

rat _____

eight _____

cat _____

bear _____

ear _____

pink _____

garden _____

playing _____

Model 5   Read these sentences.

Lesson 1

1. Yo soy un gato grande y verde con piernas largas.
2. Él es una rata naranja con ocho pelos.
3. Ella es una osa rosada con tres orejas.
4. Nosotros somos amigos. Nosotros estamos jugando en el jardín.

Translate one or more into English.

_____

_____

_____

_____

_____

_____

_____

_____

_____

Lesson 1   Translations

Fun Spanish Sentences (Model Work)

1. Yo soy un gato grande y verde con piernas largas.
2. Él es una rata naranja con ocho pelos.
3. Ella es una osa rosada con tres orejas.
4. Nosotros somos amigos. Nosotros estamos jugando en el jardín.

1. I am a big green cat with long legs.
2. He is an orange rat with eight hairs.
3. She is a pink bear with three ears.
4. We are friends. We are playing in the garden.

Translation Practice (Days 1-4)

I am a cat.	Yo soy un gato.
He is a rat.	Él es una rata.
She is a bear.	Ella es una osa.
We are in the garden.	Estamos en el jardín.

Vocabulary Review (Day 5)

rat	la rata
eight	ocho
cat	el gato
bear	el oso
ear	la oreja
pink	rosado
garden	el jardín
playing	jugando

LESSON 2

I. Verb Conjugation

Read, memorize, and copy the underlined words on the lines provided.

tener (to have)

I have	*yo* <u>tengo</u>	_____
You have	*tú* <u>tienes</u>	_____
He/She has	*él/ella/Ud.* <u>tiene</u>	_____
We have	*nosotros/(as)* <u>tenemos</u>	_____
You (all) have	*vosotros/(as)* <u>teneis</u>	_____
They have	*Uds./ellos/ellas* <u>tienen</u>	_____

II. Vocabulary

yo......I　　　　soy......I am　　　un gato......a cat

flaco......skinny　　y......and　　　verde......green

tengo......I have　　　　　　　　cuatro......four

(los) dientes......teeth　　　　　　negros......black

III. Translation Practice

Read the sentence below and repeat in Spanish. Use the vocabulary above for help.

I have four teeth.

Model I Copy the Spanish sentence(s). Draw a picture.
Lesson 2
Yo soy un gato flaco y verde. Yo tengo cuatro
dientes negros.

_____

_____

I. Verb Conjugation

Read, memorize, and copy the underlined words on the lines provided.

tener (to have)

I have	*yo* <u>tengo</u>	_____
You have	*tú* <u>tienes</u>	_____
He/She has	*él/ella/Ud.* <u>tiene</u>	_____
We have	*nosotros/(as)* <u>tenemos</u>	_____
You (all) have	*vosotros/(as)* <u>teneis</u>	_____
They have	*Uds./ellos/ellas* <u>tienen</u>	_____

II. Vocabulary

tú......you   eres......are

una rata......a rat   naranja......orange

tú......you   tienes......have

una cabeza......a head   grande......big

III. Translation Practice

Read the sentence below and repeat in Spanish. Use the vocabulary above for help.

You have a head.

Tú eres una rata naranja. Tú tienes una cabeza grande.

_____

_____

I. Verb Conjugation

Read, memorize, and copy the underlined words on the lines provided.

tener (to have)

I have	*yo* <u>tengo</u>	_____
You have	*tú* <u>tienes</u>	_____
He/She has	*él/ella/Ud.* <u>tiene</u>	_____
We have	*nosotros/(as)* <u>tenemos</u>	_____
You (all) have	*vosotros/(as)* <u>teneis</u>	_____
They have	*Uds./ellos/ellas* <u>tienen</u>	_____

II. Vocabulary

él.......he

una jirafa.......a giraffe

tiene.......has

corto.......short

es.......is

él.......he

un pescuezo.......a neck

III. Translation Practice

Read the sentence below and repeat in Spanish. Use the vocabulary above for help.

He has a neck.

Model 3 Copy the Spanish sentence(s). Draw a picture.
Lesson 2
Él es una jirafa. Él tiene un pescuezo corto.

_____

_____

I. Verb Conjugation

Read, memorize, and copy the underlined words on the lines provided.

tener (to have)

I have	*yo* tengo	_____
You have	*tú* tienes	_____
He/She has	*él/ella/Ud.* tiene	_____
We have	*nosotros/(as)* tenemos	_____
You (all) have	*vosotros/(as)* teneis	_____
They have	*Uds./ellos/ellas* tienen	_____

II. Vocabulary

nosotros......we

(los) elefantes......elephants

tenemos......we have

somos......we are

nosotros......we

pequeños......little

(los) cuerpos......bodies

III. Translation Practice

Read the sentence below and repeat in Spanish. Use the vocabulary above for help.

We have elephants.

Nosotros somos elefantes. Nosotros tenemos cuerpos pequeños.

_____

_____

Verb Conjugation Review

Write the conjugation of the verb <u>tener</u>. Use the previous page for help, if needed.

yo _____   nosotros/(as) _____

tú _____   vosotros/(as) _____

él/ella/Ud. _____   Uds./ellos/ellas _____

Vocabulary Review

Translate the following words. Remember to add the appropriate article, <u>el</u>, <u>la</u>, <u>los</u>, or <u>las</u>. Use the vocabulary from the previous pages for help, if needed.

skinny _____

head _____

neck _____

short _____

giraffe _____

green _____

elephant _____

black _____

bodies _____

teeth _____

Model 5   *Read these sentences.*

Lesson 2

1. Yo soy un gato flaco y verde. Yo tengo cuatro dientes negros.

2. Tú eres una rata naranja. Tú tienes una cabeza grande.

3. Él es una jirafa. Él tiene un pescuezo corto.

4. Nosotros somos elefantes. Nosotros tenemos cuerpos pequeños.

Translate one or more into English.

_____

_____

_____

_____

_____

_____

_____

_____

Lesson 2 Translations

Fun Spanish Sentences (Model Work)

1. Yo soy un gato flaco y verde. Yo tengo cuatro dientes negros.
2. Tú eres una rata naranja. Tú tienes una cabeza grande.
3. Él es una jirafa. Él tiene un pescuezo corto.
4. Nosotros somos elefantes. Nosotros tenemos cuerpos pequeños.

1. I am a skinny green cat. I have four black teeth.
2. You are an orange rat. You have a big head.
3. He is a giraffe. He has a short neck.
4. We are elephants. We have little bodies.

Oral Translation Practice (Days 1-4)

I have four teeth.	Yo tengo cuatro dientes.
You have a head.	Tú tienes una cabeza.
He has a neck.	Él tiene un pescuezo.
We have elephants.	Nosotros tenemos elefantes.

Vocabulary Review (Day 5)

skinny	flaco	
head	la cabeza	
neck	el pescuezo	(in humans only "el cuello")
short	baja	
giraffe	la jirafa	
green	verde	
elephant	el elefante	
black	negro	
bodies	los cuerpos	
teeth	los dientes	

LESSON 3

I. Verb Conjugation

Read, memorize, and copy the underlined words on the lines provided.

vivir (to live)

I live	*yo* <u>vivo</u>	_____
You live	*tú* <u>vives</u>	_____
He/She lives	*él/ella/Ud.* <u>vive</u>	_____
We live	*nosotros/(as)* <u>vivimos</u>	_____
You (all)	*vosotros/(as)* <u>vivis</u>	_____
They live	*Uds./ellos/ellas* <u>viven</u>	_____

II. Vocabulary

yo.......I   soy.......I am

un oso.......a bear   rosado.......pink

vivo.......I live   en.......in

una alberca.......a pool

(alberca is more for animals... la piscina is a pool for humans)

III. Translation Practice

Read the sentence below and repeat in Spanish. Use the vocabulary above for help.

I live in a pink pool.

26

Yo soy un oso rosado. Yo vivo en una alberca.

_____

_____

I. Verb Conjugation

Read, memorize, and copy the underlined words on the lines provided.

vivir (to live)

I live	*yo* <u>vivo</u>	_____
You live	*tú* <u>vives</u>	_____
He/She lives	*él/ella/Ud.* <u>vive</u>	_____
We live	*nosotros/(as)* <u>vivimos</u>	_____
You (all)	*vosotros/(as)* <u>vivis</u>	_____
They live	*Uds./ellos/ellas* <u>viven</u>	_____

II. Vocabulary

él... ..he

un caballo... ..a horse

él... ..he

en... ..in

un árbol... ..a tree

es... ..is

verde... ..green

vive... ..lives

una casa ... ..a house

III. Translation Practice

Read the sentence below and repeat in Spanish. Use the vocabulary above for help.

He lives in a house.

Model 2 Copy the Spanish sentence(s). Draw a picture.
Lesson 3

Él es un caballo verde. Él vive en una casa en un árbol.

_____

_____

I. Verb Conjugation

Read, memorize, and copy the underlined words on the lines provided.

vivir (to live)

I live	*yo* <u>vivo</u>	_____
You live	*tú* <u>vives</u>	_____
He/She lives	*él/ella/Ud.* <u>vive</u>	_____
We live	*nosotros/(as)* <u>vivimos</u>	_____
You (all)	*vosotros/(as)* <u>vivis</u>	_____
They live	*Uds./ellos/ellas* <u>viven</u>	_____

II. Vocabulary

ella... ...she

una mariposa... ...a butterfly

vive ... ...lives

el oso ... ...the bear

es... ...is

azul... ...blue

sobre... ...on

rosado... ...pink

III. Translation Practice

Read the sentence below and repeat in Spanish. Use the vocabulary above for help.

She is a pink bear.

Model 3 Copy the Spanish sentence(s). Draw a picture.
Lesson 3
Ella es una mariposa azul. Ella vive sobre el oso
rosado.

_____

_____

I. Verb Conjugation

Read, memorize, and copy the underlined words on the lines provided.

vivir (to live)

I live	*yo* <u>vivo</u>	_____
You live	*tú* <u>vives</u>	_____
He/She lives	*él/ella/Ud.* <u>vive</u>	_____
We live	*nosotros/(as)* <u>vivimos</u>	_____
You (all)	*vosotros/(as)* <u>vivís</u>	_____
They live	*Uds./ellos/ellas* <u>viven</u>	_____

II. Vocabulary

nosotros......we

(los) peces......fish

vivimos......we live

un árbol......a tree

somos......we are

y......and

en......in

III. Translation Practice

Read the sentence below and repeat in Spanish. Use the vocabulary above for help.

We live in a tree.

Model 4 *Copy the Spanish sentence(s).* *Draw a picture.*
Lesson 3

Nosotros somos peces, y vivimos en un arbol.

_____

_____

Verb Conjugation Review

Write the conjugation of the verb _vivir_. Use the previous page for help, if needed.

yo _____

tú _____

él/ella/Ud. _____

nosotros/(as) _____

vosotros/(as) _____

Uds./ellos/ellas _____

Vocabulary Review

Translate the following words. Remember to add the appropriate article, _el_, _la_, _los_, or _las_. Use the vocabulary from the previous pages for help, if needed.

tree _____

to live _____

butterfly _____

bear _____

blue _____

fish _____

pool _____

horse _____

Model 5   *Read these sentences.*

Lesson 3

1. Yo soy un oso rosado. Yo vivo en una alberca.

2. Él es un caballo verde. Él vive en una casa en un árbol.

3. Ella es una mariposa azul. Ella vive sobre el oso rosado.

4. Nosotros somos peces, y vivimos en un árbol.

Translate one or more into English.

_____

_____

_____

_____

_____

_____

_____

_____

Lesson 3 Translations

Fun Spanish Sentences (Model Work)

1. Yo soy un oso rosado. Yo vivo en una alberca.
2. Él es un caballo verde. Él vive en una casa en un árbol.
3. Ella es una mariposa azul. Ella vive sobre el oso rosado.
4. Nosotros somos peces, y vivimos en un árbol.

1. I am a pink bear. I live in a pool.
2. He is a green horse. He lives in a tree house
3. She is a blue butterfly. She lives on the pink bear.
4. We are fish, and we live in a tree.

Translation Practice (Days 1-4)

I live in a pink pool.	Yo vivo en una alberca rosada.
He lives in a house.	Él vive en una casa.
She is a pink bear.	Ella es una osa rosada.
We live in a tree.	Nosotros vivimos en un árbol.

Vocabulary Review (Day 5)

tree	el árbol
to live	vivir
butterfly	la mariposa
bear	el oso
blue	azul
fish	el pez
pool	la alberca (la piscina for humans)
horse	el caballo

LESSON 4

I. Verb Conjugation

Read, memorize, and copy the underlined words on the lines provided.

ser (to be)

I am	*yo* <u>soy</u>	_____
You are	*tú* <u>eres</u>	_____
He/She is	*él/ella/Ud.* <u>es</u>	_____
We are	*nosotros/(as)* <u>somos</u>	_____
You (all)	*vosotros/(as)* <u>sois</u>	_____
They are	*Uds./ellos/ellas* <u>son</u>	_____

II. Vocabulary

esta.......this   es.......is

una casa.......a house   azul.......blue

con.......with   siete.......seven

(los) alas....... wings   naranja.......orange

III. Translation Practice

Read the sentence below and repeat in Spanish. Use the vocabulary above for help.

This is a wing.

Lesson 4

Esta es una casa azul con siete alas naranja.

_____

_____

I. Verb Conjugation

Read, memorize, and copy the underlined words on the lines provided.

ser (to be)

I am	yo **soy**	_____
You are	tú **eres**	_____
He/She is	él/ella/Ud. **es**	_____
We are	nosotros/(as) **somos**	_____
You (all)	vosotros/(as) **sois**	_____
They are	Uds./ellos/ellas **son**	_____

II. Vocabulary

este......this

un caballo......a horse

con......with

(las) alas......wings

es......is

gris......grey

dos......two

rojas......red

III. Translation Practice

Read the sentence below and repeat in Spanish. Use the vocabulary above for help.

This is a red horse.

Model 2 Copy the Spanish sentence(s). Draw a picture.
Lesson 4

Este es un caballo gris con dos alas rojas.

_____

_____

I. Verb Conjugation

Read, memorize, and copy the underlined words on the lines provided.

ser (to be)

I am	*yo* <u>soy</u>	_____
You are	*tú* <u>eres</u>	_____
He/She is	*él/ella/Ud.* <u>es</u>	_____
We are	*nosotros/(as)* <u>somos</u>	_____
You (all)	*vosotros/(as)* <u>sois</u>	_____
They are	*Uds./ellos/ellas* <u>son</u>	_____

II. Vocabulary

este.....this   es.....is   un pez.....a fish

rosado.....pink   con.....with

nueve.....nine   (las) alas.....wings

negras.....black

III. Translation Practice

Read the sentence below and repeat in Spanish. Use the vocabulary above for help.

This is a fish,

Model 3 Copy the Spanish sentence(s). Draw a picture.
Lesson 4
Este es un pez rosado con nueve alas negras.

_____

_____

I. Verb Conjugation

Read, memorize, and copy the underlined words on the lines provided.

ser (to be)

I am	*yo* **soy**	_____
You are	*tú* **eres**	_____
He/She is	*él/ella/Ud.* **es**	_____
We are	*nosotros/(as)* **somos**	_____
You (all)	*vosotros/(as)* **sois**	_____
They are	*Uds./ellos/ellas* **son**	_____

II. Vocabulary

el caballo......the horse

y......and

están......they are (temp. condition)

sobre......over

azules......blue

el pez......the fish

la casa......the house

volando......flying

los árboles......the trees

(volar......fly)

III. Translation Practice

Read the sentence below and repeat in Spanish. Use the vocabulary above for help.

They are flying over the tree.   (Ellos... They)

Model 4 Copy the Spanish sentence(s). Draw a picture.
Lesson 4
El caballo, el pez y la casa están volando sobre
los árboles azules.

_____

_____

Verb Conjugation Review

Write the conjugation of the verb _ser_. Use the previous page for help, if needed.

yo _____   nosotros/(as) _____

tú _____   vosotros/(as) _____

él/ella/Ud. _____   Uds./ellos/ellas _____

Vocabulary Review

Translate the following words. Remember to add the appropriate article, _el_, _la_, _los_, or _las_. Use the vocabulary from the previous pages for help, if needed.

seven   _____

gray   _____

wings   _____

trees   _____

two   _____

this   _____

and   _____

flying   _____

Model 5   Read these sentences.

Lesson 4

1. Esta es una casa azul con siete alas naranja.

2. Este es un caballo gris con dos alas rojas.

3. Este es un pez rosado con nueve alas negras.

4. El caballo, el pez y la casa están volando sobre los árboles azules.

Translate one or more into English.

_____

_____

_____

_____

_____

_____

_____

_____

_____

Lesson 4   Translations

Fun Spanish Sentences (Model Work)

1. Esta es una casa azul con siete alas naranja.
2. Este es un caballo gris con dos alas rojas.
3. Este es un pez rosado con nueve alas negras.
4. El caballo, el pez y la casa están volando sobre los árboles azules.

1. This is a blue house with seven orange wings.
2. This is a gray horse with two red wings.
3. This is a pink fish with nine black wings.
4. The horse, fish, and house are flying over the blue trees.

Translation Practice (Days 1-4)

This is a wing.	Esta es un ala.
This is a red horse.	Este es un caballo rojo.
This is a fish.	Este es un pez.
They are flying over the tree.	Ellos están volando sobre el árbol.

Vocabulary Review (Day 5)

seven	siete
gray	gris
wings	las alas
trees	los árboles
two	dos
this	este
and	y
flying	volando

LESSON 5

I. Verb Conjugation

Read, memorize, and copy the underlined words on the lines provided.

comer (to eat)

I eat	*yo* <u>como</u>	_____
You eat	*tú* <u>comes</u>	_____
He/She eats	*él/ella/Ud.* <u>come</u>	_____
We eat	*nosotros/(as)* <u>comemos</u>	_____
You (all)	*vosotros/(as)* <u>comeis</u>	_____
They eat	*Uds./ellos/ellas* <u>comen</u>	_____

II. Vocabulary

esos... ...those   (los) perros... ...dogs
azules... ..blue   juegan... ..play
en... ..in   un tazón... ...a bowl
de... ..of   (la) leche... ...milk

III. Translation Practice

Read the sentence below and repeat in Spanish. Use the vocabulary above for help.

Those dogs play in the milk.

Model / Copy the Spanish sentence(s). Draw a picture.
Lesson 5
Esos perros azules juegan en un tazón de leche.

_____

_____

I. Verb Conjugation

Read, memorize, and copy the underlined words on the lines provided.

comer (to eat)

I eat	*yo* <u>como</u>	_____
You eat	*tú* <u>comes</u>	_____
He/She eats	*él/ella/Ud.* <u>come</u>	_____
We eat	*nosotros/(as)* <u>comemos</u>	_____
You (all)	*vosotros/(as)* <u>comeis</u>	_____
They eat	*Uds./ellos/ellas* <u>comen</u>	_____

II. Vocabulary

esos......those

rojos......red

detrás de......behind

(los) perros......dogs

bailan......dance

el garaje......garage

del is a contraction of de and el

III. Translation Practice

Read the sentence below and repeat in Spanish. Use the vocabulary above for help.

Those dogs dance behind those red dogs.

Model 2 Copy the Spanish sentence(s). Draw a picture.
Lesson 5
Esos perros rojos bailan detrás del garaje.

_____

_____

I. Verb Conjugation

Read, memorize, and copy the underlined words on the lines provided.

comer (to eat)

English	Spanish	
I eat	*yo* <u>como</u>	_____
You eat	*tú* <u>comes</u>	_____
He/She eats	*él/ella/Ud.* <u>come</u>	_____
We eat	*nosotros/(as)* <u>comemos</u>	_____
You (all)	*vosotros/(as)* <u>comeis</u>	_____
They eat	*Uds./ellos/ellas* <u>comen</u>	_____

II. Vocabulary

esos... ...those

naranja... ...orange

sobre... ...over

roja... ...red

(los) conejos... ...rabbits

vuelan... ...fly

la casa... ...the house

III. Translation Practice

Read the sentence below and repeat in Spanish. Use the vocabulary above for help.

Those rabbits fly over the house.

Model 3 Copy the Spanish sentence(s). Draw a picture.
Lesson 5
Esos conejos naranja vuelan sobre la casa roja.

_____

_____

I. Verb Conjugation

Read, memorize, and copy the underlined words on the lines provided.

comer (to eat)

I eat	*yo* <u>como</u>	_____
You eat	*tú* <u>comes</u>	_____
He/She eats	*él/ella/Ud.* <u>come</u>	_____
We eat	*nosotros/(as)* <u>comemos</u>	_____
You (all)	*vosotros/(as)* <u>comeis</u>	_____
They eat	*Uds./ellos/ellas* <u>comen</u>	_____

II. Vocabulary

esos.......those

(los) conejos......rabbits

en frente de......in front of

la ventana......the window

pequeños......little

comen......eat

III. Translation Practice

Read the sentence below and repeat in Spanish. Use the vocabulary above for help.

Those rabbits eat in front of the window.

Model 4 Copy the Spanish sentence(s). Draw a picture.
Lesson 5
Esos pequeños conejos comen en frente de la ventana.

_____

_____

Verb Conjugation Review

Write the conjugation of the verb <u>comer</u>. Use the previous page for help, if needed.

yo _____   nosotros/(as) _____

tú _____   vosotros/(as) _____

él/ella/Ud. _____   Uds./ellos/ellas _____

Vocabulary Review

Translate the following words. Remember to add the appropriate article, <u>el</u>, <u>la</u>, <u>los</u>, or <u>las</u>. Use the vocabulary from the previous pages for help, if needed.

window   _____

dogs   _____

rabbits   _____

milk   _____

house   _____

bowl   _____

garage   _____

in front of   _____

little   _____

Model 5   *Read these sentences.*

Lesson 5

1. Esos perros azules juegan en un tazón de leche.
2. Esos perros rojos bailan detrás del garaje.
3. Esos conejos naranja vuelan sobre la casa roja.
4. Esos pequeños conejos comen en frente de la ventana.

Translate one or more into English.

_____

_____

_____

_____

_____

_____

_____

_____

Lesson 5   Translations

Fun Spanish Sentences (Model Work)

1. Esos perros azules juegan en un tazón de leche.
2. Esos perros rojos bailan detrás del garaje.
3. Esos conejos naranja vuelan sobre la casa roja.
4. Esos pequeños conejos comen en frente de la ventana.

1. Those blue dogs play in a bowl of milk.
2. Those red dogs dance behind the garage.
3. Those orange rabbits fly over the red house.
4. Those little rabbits eat in front of the window.

Translation Practice (Days 1-4)

Those dogs play in the milk.	Esos perros juegan en la leche.
Those dogs dance behind those red dogs.	Esos perros bailan detrás de esos perros rojos.
Those rabbits fly over the house.	Esos conejos vuelan sobre la casa.
Those rabbits eat in front of the window.	Esos conejos comen en frente de la ventana.

Vocabulary Review (Day 5)

window	la ventana
dogs	perros
rabbits	los conejos
milk	jugar
house	bailar
bowl	un tazón
garage	el garaje
in front of	en frente de
little	pequeño

LESSON 6

I. Verb Conjugation

Read, memorize, and copy the underlined words on the lines provided.

comer (to eat)

I eat	*yo* <u>como</u>	_____
You eat	*tú* <u>comes</u>	_____
He/She eats	*él/ella/Ud.* <u>come</u>	_____
We eat	*nosotros/(as)* <u>comemos</u>	_____
You (all)	*vosotros/(as)* <u>comeis</u>	_____
They eat	*Uds./ellos/ellas* <u>comen</u>	_____

II. Vocabulary

yo... .. I

un pajáro... ...bird

como... ... I eat

morados... ...purple

soy... ...I am

amarillo... ...yellow

(los) gusanos... ...worms

III. Translation Practice

Read the sentence below and repeat in Spanish. Use the vocabulary above for help.

I am a worm.

Model I Copy the Spanish sentence(s). Draw a picture.
Lesson 6

Yo soy un pájaro amarillo. Yo como gusanos morados.

_____

_____

I. Verb Conjugation

Read, memorize, and copy the underlined words on the lines provided.

comer (to eat)

I eat	*yo* <u>como</u>	_____
You eat	*tú* <u>comes</u>	_____
He/She eats	*él/ella/Ud.* <u>come</u>	_____
We eat	*nosotros/(as)* <u>comemos</u>	_____
You (all)	*vosotros/(as)* <u>comeis</u>	_____
They eat	*Uds./ellos/ellas* <u>comen</u>	_____

II. Vocabulary

él......he   es......is

una rana......a frog   roja......red

él......he   come......eats

(las) moscas......flies

III. Translation Practice

Read the sentence below and repeat in Spanish. Use the vocabulary above for help.

The fly eats frogs.

Model 2 Copy the Spanish sentence(s). Draw a picture.
Lesson 6

Él es una rana roja. Él come moscas.

_____

_____

I. Verb Conjugation

Read, memorize, and copy the underlined words on the lines provided.

comer (to eat)

I eat	*yo* <u>como</u>	_____
You eat	*tú* <u>comes</u>	_____
He/She eats	*él/ella/Ud.* <u>come</u>	_____
We eat	*nosotros/(as)* <u>comemos</u>	_____
You (all)	*vosotros/(as)* <u>comeis</u>	_____
They eat	*Uds./ellos/ellas* <u>comen</u>	_____

II. Vocabulary

nosotros.....we

(los) monos.....monkeys

comemos.....we eat

somos.....we are

amarillos.....yellow

(los) fideos.....pasta

III. Translation Practice

Read the sentence below and repeat in Spanish. Use the vocabulary above for help.

The monkeys eat pasta.

Model 3 Copy the Spanish sentence(s). Draw a picture.
Lesson 6
Nosotros somos monos amarillos. Nosotros comemos fideos.

_____

_____

I. Verb Conjugation

Read, memorize, and copy the underlined words on the lines provided.

comer (to eat)

I eat	*yo* <u>como</u>	_____
You eat	*tú* <u>comes</u>	_____
He/She eats	*él/ella/Ud.* <u>come</u>	_____
We eat	*nosotros/(as)* <u>comemos</u>	_____
You (all)	*vosotros/(as)* <u>comeis</u>	_____
They eat	*Uds./ellos/ellas* <u>comen</u>	_____

II. Vocabulary

ellos......they

tiburones......sharks

ellos......they

frijoles......beans

son......are

rojos......red

comen......eat

III. Translation Practice

Read the sentence below and repeat in Spanish. Use the vocabulary above for help.

Sharks eat beans.

Model 4 Copy the Spanish sentence(s). Draw a picture.
Lesson 6
Ellos son tiburones rojos. Ellos comen frijoles.

_____

_____

Verb Conjugation Review

Write the conjugation of the verb <u>comer</u>. Use the previous page for help, if needed.

yo _____   nosotros/(as) _____

tú _____   vosotros/(as) _____

él/ella/Ud. _____   Uds./ellos/ellas _____

Vocabulary Review

Translate the following words. Remember to add the appropriate article, <u>el</u>, <u>la</u>, <u>los</u>, or <u>las</u>. Use the vocabulary from the previous pages for help, if needed.

bird   _____

worm   _____

flies   _____

beans   _____

yellow   _____

monkeys   _____

sharks   _____

frog   _____

purple   _____

pasta   _____

Model 5   *Read these sentences.*

Lesson 6

1. Yo soy un pájaro amarillo. Yo como gusanos morados.

2. Él es una rana roja. Él come moscas.

3. Nosotros somos monos amarillos. Nosotros comemos fideos.

4. Ellos son tiburones rojos. Ellos comen frijoles.

Translate one or more into English.

_____

_____

_____

_____

_____

_____

_____

_____

Lesson 6   Translations

Fun Spanish Sentences (Model Work)

1. Yo soy un pájaro amarillo. Yo como gusanos morados.
2. Él es una rana roja. Él come moscas.
3. Nosotros somos monos amarillos. Nosotros comemos fideos.
4. Ellos son tiburones rojos. Ellos comen frijoles.

1. I am a yellow bird. I eat purple worms.
2. He is a red frog. He eats flies.
3. We are yellow monkeys. We eat pasta.
4. They are red sharks. They eat beans.

Translation Practice (Days 1-4)

I am a worm.	Yo soy un gusano.
The fly eats frogs.	La mosca come ranas.
The monkeys eat pasta.	Los monos comen fideos.
Sharks eat beans.	Los tiburones comen frijoles.

Vocabulary Review (Day 5)

bird	el pájaro
worm	el gusano
flies	las moscas
beans	los frijoles
yellow	amarillo
monkeys	los monos
sharks	los tiburones
frog	la rana
purple	morado
pasta	los fideos

LESSON 7

I. Verb Conjugation

Read, memorize, and copy the underlined words on the lines provided.

jugar (to play)

I play	*yo* <u>juego</u>	_____
You play	*tú* <u>juegas</u>	_____
He/She plays	*él/ella/Ud.* <u>juega</u>	_____
We play	*nosotros/(as)* <u>jugamos</u>	_____
You (all) play	*vosotros/(as)* <u>jugáis</u>	_____
They play	*Uds./ellos/ellas* <u>juegan</u>	_____

II. Vocabulary

yo......I

una vaca......cow

feliz......happy

en......in

soy......I am

roja......red

juego......I play

la arena......the sand

III. Translation Practice

Read the sentence below and repeat in Spanish. Use the vocabulary above for help.

I am a red cow.

Model 1 Copy the Spanish sentence(s). Draw a picture.
Lesson 7

Yo soy una vaca roja feliz. Yo juego en la arena.

_____

_____

I. Verb Conjugation

Read, memorize, and copy the underlined words on the lines provided.

jugar (to play)

I play	*yo* <u>juego</u>	_____
You play	*tú* <u>juegas</u>	_____
He/She plays	*él/ella/Ud.* <u>juega</u>	_____
We play	*nosotros/(as)* <u>jugamos</u>	_____
You (all) play	*vosotros/(as)* <u>jugáis</u>	_____
They play	*Uds./ellos/ellas* <u>juegan</u>	_____

II. Vocabulary

ella......she

una pata......a duck

enojada......angry

en......on

es......is

morada......purple

juega......plays

el tobogán......the slide

III. Translation Practice

Read the sentence below and repeat in Spanish. Use the vocabulary above for help.

She is a duck.

Model 2 Copy the Spanish sentence(s). Draw a picture.
Lesson 7
Ella es una pata morada enojada. Ella juega en
el tobogán.

_____

_____

I. Verb Conjugation

Read, memorize, and copy the underlined words on the lines provided.

jugar (to play)

I play	*yo* <u>juego</u>	_____
You play	*tú* <u>juegas</u>	_____
He/She plays	*él/ella/Ud.* <u>juega</u>	_____
We play	*nosotros/(as)* <u>jugamos</u>	_____
You (all) play	*vosotros/(as)* <u>jugáis</u>	_____
They play	*Uds./ellos/ellas* <u>juegan</u>	_____

II. Vocabulary

ellas......they

(las) ovejas......sheep

tristes......sad

en......on

son......are

negras......black

juegan......plan

el techo......the roof

III. Translation Practice

Read the sentence below and repeat in Spanish. Use the vocabulary above for help.

The sheep are black.

Model 3 Copy the Spanish sentence(s). Draw a picture.
Lesson 7

Ellas son ovejas negras tristes. Ellas juegan en el techo.

_____

_____

I. Verb Conjugation

Read, memorize, and copy the underlined words on the lines provided.

jugar (to play)

I play	*yo* <u>juego</u>	_____
You play	*tú* <u>juegas</u>	_____
He/She plays	*él/ella/Ud.* <u>juega</u>	_____
We play	*nosotros/(as)* <u>jugamos</u>	_____
You (all) play	*vosotros/(as)* <u>jugáis</u>	_____
They play	*Uds./ellos/ellas* <u>juegan</u>	_____

II. Vocabulary

nosotros.....we   jugamos.....we play

en.....in   el parque.....the park

en.....in   la lluvia.....the rain

III. Translation Practice

Read the sentence below and repeat in Spanish. Use the vocabulary above for help.

We play in the rain.

Model 4 Copy the Spanish sentence(s). Draw a picture.
Lesson 7
Nosotros jugamos en el parque en la lluvia.

_____

_____

Verb Conjugation Review

Write the conjugation of the verb _jugar_. Use the previous page for help, if needed.

yo _____   nosotros/(as) _____

tú _____   vosotros/(as) _____

él/ella/Ud. _____   Uds./ellos/ellas _____

Vocabulary Review

Translate the following words. Remember to add the appropriate article, _el_, _la_, _los_, or _las_. Use the vocabulary from the previous pages for help, if needed.

cow _____

duck _____

angry _____

slide _____

sheep _____

park _____

sand _____

roof _____

rain _____

happy _____

sad _____

Model 5   *Read these sentences.*

Lesson 7

1. Yo soy una vaca roja feliz. Yo juego en la arena.

2. Ella es una pata morada enojada. Ella juega en el tobogán.

3. Ellas son ovejas negras tristes. Ellas juegan en el techo.

4. Nosotros jugamos en el parque en la lluvia.

Translate one or more into English.

_____

_____

_____

_____

_____

_____

_____

Lesson 7   Translations

Fun Spanish Sentences (Model Work)

1. Yo soy una vaca roja feliz. Yo juego en la arena.
2. Ella es una pata morada enojada. Ella juega en el tobogán.
3. Ellas son ovejas negras tristes. Ellas juegan en el techo.
4. Nosotros jugamos en el parque en la lluvia.

1. I am a happy red cow. I play in the sand.
2. She is an angry purple duck. She plays on the slide.
3. They are sad black sheep. They play on the roof.
4. We play in the park in the rain.

Translation Practice (Days 1-4)

I am a red cow.	Yo soy una vaca roja.
She is a duck.	Ella es una pata.
The sheep are black.	Las ovejas son negras.
We play in the rain.	Nosotros jugamos en la lluvia.

Vocabulary Review (Day 5)

cow	la vaca
duck	un(a) pato(a)
angry	enojado(a)
slide	el tobogán
sheep	la oveja
park	el parque
sand	la arena
roof	el techo
rain	la lluvia
happy	feliz
sad	triste

LESSON 8

I. Verb Conjugation

Read, memorize, and copy the underlined words on the lines provided.

saltar (to jump)

I jump	*yo* <u>salto</u>	_____
You jump	*tú* <u>saltas</u>	_____
He/She jumps	*él/ella/Ud.* <u>salta</u>	_____
We jump	*nosotros/(as)* <u>saltamos</u>	_____
You (all) jump	*vosotros/(as)* <u>saltais</u>	_____
They jump	*Uds./ellos/ellas* <u>saltan</u>	_____

II. Vocabulary

yo......I

una gallina......a chicken

sobre......over

soy......I am

salto......I jump

la mesa......the table

III. Translation Practice

Read the sentence below and repeat in Spanish. Use the vocabulary above for help.

I jump over the chicken.

Model / Copy the Spanish sentence(s). Draw a picture.
Lesson 8
Yo soy una gallina. Yo salto sobre la mesa.

_____

_____

I. Verb Conjugation

Read, memorize, and copy the underlined words on the lines provided.

saltar (to jump)

I jump	*yo* <u>salto</u>	_____
You jump	*tú* <u>saltas</u>	_____
He/She jumps	*él/ella/Ud.* <u>salta</u>	_____
We jump	*nosotros/(as)* <u>saltamos</u>	_____
You (all) jump	*vosotros/(as)* <u>saltais</u>	_____
They jump	*Uds./ellos/ellas* <u>saltan</u>	_____

II. Vocabulary

él.......he

una rana.......a frog

en.......on

es.......is

salta.......jumps

el sofá.......the sofa

III. Translation Practice

Read the sentence below and repeat in Spanish. Use the vocabulary above for help.

He jumps on the frog.

Model 2 Copy the Spanish sentence(s). Draw a picture.
Lesson 8
Él es una rana. Él salta en el sofá.

I. Verb Conjugation

Read, memorize, and copy the underlined words on the lines provided.

saltar (to jump)

I jump	*yo* <u>salto</u>	_____
You jump	*tú* <u>saltas</u>	_____
He/She jumps	*él/ella/Ud.* <u>salta</u>	_____
We jump	*nosotros/(as)* <u>saltamos</u>	_____
You (all) jump	*vosotros/(as)* <u>saltais</u>	_____
They jump	*Uds./ellos/ellas* <u>saltan</u>	_____

II. Vocabulary

ella......she

un ratón......mouse

en......on

es......is

salta......jumps

la cama......the bed

III. Translation Practice

Read the sentence below and repeat in Spanish. Use the vocabulary above for help.

A mouse jumps on the bed.

Model 3 Copy the Spanish sentence(s). Draw a picture.
Lesson 8
Ella es un ratón. Ella salta en la cama.

I. Verb Conjugation

Read, memorize, and copy the underlined words on the lines provided.

saltar (to jump)

I jump	*yo* <u>salto</u>	_____
You jump	*tú* <u>saltas</u>	_____
He/She jumps	*él/ella/Ud.* <u>salta</u>	_____
We jump	*nosotros/(as)* <u>saltamos</u>	_____
You (all) jump	*vosotros/(as)* <u>saltais</u>	_____
They jump	*Uds./ellos/ellas* <u>saltan</u>	_____

II. Vocabulary

nosotros……we
sobre……over

saltamos……we jump
la luna……the moon

III. Translation Practice

Read the sentence below and repeat in Spanish. Use the vocabulary above for help.

We jump the moon.

Model 4 Copy the Spanish sentence(s). Draw a picture.
Lesson 8

Nosotros saltamos sobre la luna.

_____

_____

Verb Conjugation Review

Write the conjugation of the verb <u>saltar</u>. Use the previous page for help, if needed.

yo _____   nosotros/(as) _____

tú _____   vosotros/(as) _____

él/ella/Ud. _____   Uds./ellos/ellas _____

Vocabulary Review

Translate the following words. Remember to add the appropriate article, <u>el</u>, <u>la</u>, <u>los</u>, or <u>las</u>. Use the vocabulary from the previous pages for help, if needed.

chicken   _____

table   _____

sofa   _____

mouse   _____

bed   _____

moon   _____

over   _____

frog   _____

jump   _____

Model 5   *Read these sentences.*

Lesson 8

1. Yo soy una gallina. Yo salto sobre la mesa.
2. Él es una rana. El salta en el sofá
3. Ella es un ratón. Ella salta en la cama.
4. Nosotros saltamos sobre la luna.

Translate one or more into English.

_____

_____

_____

_____

_____

_____

_____

_____

Lesson 8   Translations

Fun Spanish Sentences (Model Work)

1. Yo soy una gallina. Yo salto sobre la mesa.
2. Él es una rana. El salta en el sofá.
3. Ella es un ratón. Ella salta en la cama.
4. Nosotros saltamos sobre la luna.

1. I am a chicken. I jump over the table.
2. He is a frog. He jumps on the sofa.
3. She is a mouse. She jumps on the bed.
4. We jump over the moon.

Translation Practice (Days 1-4)

I jump over the chicken.	Yo salto sobre la gallina.
He jumps on the frog.	El salta en la rana.
A mouse jumps on the bed.	Un ratón salta en la cama.
We jump the moon.	Nosotros saltamos la luna.

Vocabulary Review (Day 5)

chicken	la gallina
table	la mesa
sofa	el sofá
mouse	el ratón
bed	la cama
moon	la luna
over	sobre
frog	la rana
to jump	saltar

LESSON 9

I. Verb Conjugation

Read, memorize, and copy the underlined words on the lines provided.

ver (to see)

I see	yo <u>veo</u>	_____
You see	tú <u>ves</u>	_____
He/She sees	él/ella/Ud. <u>ve</u>	_____
We see	nosotros/(as) <u>vemos</u>	_____
You (all) see	vosotros/(as) <u>veis</u>	_____
They see	Uds./ellos/ellas <u>ven</u>	_____

II. Vocabulary

yo......I

cinco......five

grandes......big

veo......I see

(los) huevos......eggs

en......in

el nido.. the nest

(el nido is also used for nest)

III. Translation Practice

Read the sentence below and repeat in Spanish. Use the vocabulary above for help.

I see eggs.

Model I Copy the Spanish sentence(s). Draw a picture.
Lesson 9
Yo veo cinco huevos grandes en el nido.

———————————————————————————

———————————————————————————

I. Verb Conjugation

Read, memorize, and copy the underlined words on the lines provided.

ver (to see)

I see	*yo* <u>veo</u>	_____
You see	*tú* <u>ves</u>	_____
He/She sees	*él/ella/Ud.* <u>ve</u>	_____
We see	*nosotros/(as)* <u>vemos</u>	_____
You (all) see	*vosotros/(as)* <u>veis</u>	_____
They see	*Uds./ellos/ellas* <u>ven</u>	_____

II. Vocabulary

tú......you

diez......ten

pequeños......little

el techo......the roof

ves......see

(los) huevos......eggs

en......on

III. Translation Practice

Read the sentence below and repeat in Spanish. Use the vocabulary above for help.

You see eggs on the roof.

Model 2 Copy the Spanish sentence(s). Draw a picture.
Lesson 9
Tú ves diez huevos pequeños en el techo.

_____

_____

I. Verb Conjugation

Read, memorize, and copy the underlined words on the lines provided.

ver (to see)

I see	*yo* **veo**	_____
You see	*tú* **ves**	_____
He/She sees	*él/ella/Ud.* **ve**	_____
We see	*nosotros/(as)* **vemos**	_____
You (all) see	*vosotros/(as)* **veis**	_____
They see	*Uds./ellos/ellas* **ven**	_____

II. Vocabulary

él......he	ve......sees
un......one	un huevo......one egg
caer......fall	del techo......from the roof

del is a contraction of de and el

III. Translation Practice

Read the sentence below and repeat in Spanish. Use the vocabulary above for help.

He sees the roof.

Model 3 Copy the Spanish sentence(s). Draw a picture.

Lesson 9

Él ve un huevo caer del techo.

_____

_____

I. Verb Conjugation

Read, memorize, and copy the underlined words on the lines provided.

ver (to see)

I see	*yo* **veo**	_____
You see	*tú* **ves**	_____
He/She sees	*él/ella/Ud.* **ve**	_____
We see	*nosotros/(as)* **vemos**	_____
You (all) see	*vosotros/(as)* **veis**	_____
They see	*Uds./ellos/ellas* **ven**	_____

II. Vocabulary

nosotros.....we

un dinosaurio.....a dinosaur

en.....on

vemos.....we see

sentando.....sitting

el huevo.....the egg

III. Translation Practice

Read the sentence below and repeat in Spanish. Use the vocabulary above for help.

We see a dinosaur.

Model 4 Copy the Spanish sentence(s). Draw a picture.
Lesson 9

Nosotros vemos un dinosaurio sentando en el huevo.

_____

_____

Verb Conjugation Review

Write the conjugation of the verb <u>ver</u>. Use the previous page for help, if needed.

yo _____   nosotros/(as) _____

tú _____   vosotros/(as) _____

él/ella/Ud._____   Uds./ellos/ellas _____

Vocabulary Review

Translate the following words. Remember to add the appropriate article, <u>el</u>, <u>la</u>, <u>los</u>, or <u>las</u>. Use the vocabulary from the previous pages for help, if needed.

five   _____

eggs   _____

nest   _____

ten   _____

little   _____

fall   _____

dinosaur   _____

roof   _____

sitting   _____

Model 5   *Read these sentences.*
Lesson 9
1. Yo veo cinco huevos grandes en el nido.
2. Tú ves diez huevos pequeños en el techo.
3. El ve un huevo caer del techo.
4. Nosotros vemos un dinosaurio sentando en el huevo.

Translate one or more into English.

_____

_____

_____

_____

_____

_____

_____

_____

Lesson 9   Translations

Fun Spanish Sentences (Model Work)

1. I see five big eggs in the nest.
2. You see ten little eggs on the roof.
3. He sees one egg fall from the roof.
4. We see a dinosaur sitting on the egg.

1. Yo veo cinco huevos grandes en el nido.
2. Tú ves diez huevos pequeños en el techo.
3. El ve un huevo caer del techo.
4. Nosotros vemos un dinosaurio sentando en el huevo.

Translation Practice (Days 1-4)

I see eggs.	Yo veo huevos.
You see eggs on the roof.	Tú ves huevos en el techo.
He sees the roof.	El ve el techo.
We see a dinosaur.	Nosotros vemos un dinosaurio.

Vocabulary Review (Day 5)

five	cinco
eggs	los huevos
nest	el nido
ten	diez
little	pequeño
fall	caer
dinosaur	el dinosaurio
roof	el techo
sitting	sentando

LESSON 10

I. Verb Conjugation

Read, memorize, and copy the underlined words on the lines provided.

oír (to hear)

I hear	yo <u>oigo</u>	_____
You hear	tú <u>oyes</u>	_____
He/She hears	él/ella/Ud. <u>oye</u>	_____
We hear	nosotros/(as) <u>oímos</u>	_____
You (all) hear	vosotros/(as) <u>oís</u>	_____
They hear	Uds./ellos/ellas <u>oyen</u>	_____

II. Vocabulary

yo......I

(los) cocodrilos......crocodiles

de......from

(caer.....fall)

oigo......I hear

cayendo......falling

los árboles......the trees

III. Translation Practice

Read the sentence below and repeat in Spanish. Use the vocabulary above for help.

I hear crocodiles.

Model 1 Copy the Spanish sentence(s). Draw a picture.
Lesson 10
Yo oigo cocodrilos cayendo de los árboles.

_____

_____

I. Verb Conjugation

Read, memorize, and copy the underlined words on the lines provided.

oír (to hear)

I hear	yo **oigo**	_____
You hear	tú **oyes**	_____
He/She hears	él/ella/Ud. **oye**	_____
We hear	nosotros/(as) **oímos**	_____
You (all) hear	vosotros/(as) **oís**	_____
They hear	Uds./ellos/ellas **oyen**	_____

II. Vocabulary

tú..….you

(los) pavos..…..turkeys

un libro..…..a book

oyes..…..you hear

leyendo..…..reading

(leer..…..read)

III. Translation Practice

Read the sentence below and repeat in Spanish. Use the vocabulary above for help.

You hear turkeys.

Model 2 Copy the Spanish sentence(s). Draw a picture.
Lesson 10
Tú oyes pavos leyendo un libro.

_____

_____

I. Verb Conjugation

Read, memorize, and copy the underlined words on the lines provided.

oír (to hear)

I hear	yo <u>oigo</u>	_____
You hear	tú <u>oyes</u>	_____
He/She hears	él/ella/Ud. <u>oye</u>	_____
We hear	nosotros/(as) <u>oímos</u>	_____
You (all) hear	vosotros/(as) <u>oís</u>	_____
They hear	Uds./ellos/ellas <u>oyen</u>	_____

II. Vocabulary

ella......she

(los) perros......the dogs

una canción......a song

oye......she hears

cantando......singing

(cantar......sing)

III. Translation Practice

Read the sentence below and repeat in Spanish. Use the vocabulary above for help.

She hears dogs.

Model 3 Copy the Spanish sentence(s). Draw a picture.
Lesson 10
Ella oye perros cantando una canción.

_____

_____

I. Verb Conjugation

Read, memorize, and copy the underlined words on the lines provided.

oír (to hear)

I hear	yo <u>oigo</u>	_____
You hear	tú <u>oyes</u>	_____
He/She hears	él/ella/Ud. <u>oye</u>	_____
We hear	nosotros/(as) <u>oímos</u>	_____
You (all) hear	vosotros/(as) <u>oís</u>	_____
They hear	Uds./ellos/ellas <u>oyen</u>	_____

II. Vocabulary

ellos......they
(los) pollos......chickens
por......through
(run......correr)

oyen......hear
corriendo......running
la cocina......the kitchen

III. Translation Practice

Read the sentence below and repeat in Spanish. Use the vocabulary above for help.

They hear chickens.

Model 4 Copy the Spanish sentence(s). Draw a picture.
Lesson 10
Ellos oyen pollos corriendo por la cocina.

_____

_____

Verb Conjugation Review

Write the conjugation of the verb _oír_. Use the previous page for help, if needed.

yo _____   nosotros/(as) _____

tú _____   vosotros/(as) _____

él/ella/Ud._____   Uds./ellos/ellas _____

Vocabulary Review

Translate the following words. Remember to add the appropriate article, _el_, _la_, _los_, or _las_. Use the vocabulary from the previous pages for help, if needed.

to hear   _____

turkey   _____

book   _____

reading   _____

kitchen   _____

through   _____

singing   _____

running   _____

Model 5   *Read these sentences.*
Lesson 10
1. Yo oigo cocodrilos cayendo de los árboles.
2. Tú oyes pavos leyendo un libro.
3. Ella oye perros cantando una canción.
4. Ellos oyen pollos corriendo por la cocina.

Translate one or more into English.

_____

_____

_____

_____

_____

_____

_____

_____

Lesson 10 Translations

Fun Spanish Sentences (Model Work)

1. Yo oigo cocodrilos cayendo de los árboles.
2. Tú oyes pavos leyendo un libro.
3. Ella oye perros cantando una canción.
4. Ellos oyen pollos corriendo por la cocina.

1. I hear crocodiles falling from the trees.
2. You hear turkeys reading a book.
3. She hears dogs singing a song.
4. They hear chickens running through the kitchen.

Translation Practice (Days 1-4)

I hear crocodiles.	Yo oigo cocodrilos.
You hear turkeys.	Tú oyes pavos.
She hears dogs.	Ella oye perros.
They hear chickens.	Ellos oyen pollos.

Vocabulary Review (Day 5)

to hear	oír
turkey	el pavo
book	el libro
reading	leyendo
kitchen	la cocina
through	por
singing	cantando
running	corriendo

LESSON 11

I. Verb Conjugation

Read, memorize, and copy the underlined words on the lines provided.

	dormir (to sleep)	
I sleep	*yo* <u>duermo</u>	_____
You sleep	*tú* <u>duermes</u>	_____
He/She sleeps	*él/ella/Ud.* <u>duerme</u>	_____
We sleep	*nosotros/(as)* <u>dormimos</u>	_____
You (all) sleep	*vosotros/(as)* <u>dormís</u>	_____
They sleep	*Uds./ellos/ellas* <u>duermen</u>	_____

II. Vocabulary

yo......I

pequeño......little

duermo......sleep

una flor.....a flower

soy......I am

(el) abejón......bumblebee

en......in

III. Translation Practice

Read the sentence below and repeat in Spanish. Use the vocabulary above for help.

I am a little flower.

Lesson 11

Yo soy un pequeño abejón. Yo duermo en una flor.

_____

_____

I. Verb Conjugation

Read, memorize, and copy the underlined words on the lines provided.

dormir (to sleep)

I sleep	yo <u>duermo</u>	_____
You sleep	tú <u>duermes</u>	_____
He/She sleeps	él/ella/Ud. <u>duerme</u>	_____
We sleep	nosotros/(as) <u>dormimos</u>	_____
You (all) sleep	vosotros/(as) <u>dormís</u>	_____
They sleep	Uds./ellos/ellas <u>duermen</u>	_____

II. Vocabulary

tú.....you

un burro.....a donkey

duermes.....you sleep

una flor.....a flower

eres.....are

blanco.....white

en.....in

III. Translation Practice

Read the sentence below and repeat in Spanish. Use the vocabulary above for help.

You are a white flower.

Model 2 Copy the Spanish sentence(s). Draw a picture.
Lesson 11
Tú eres un burro blanco. Tú duermes en una flor.

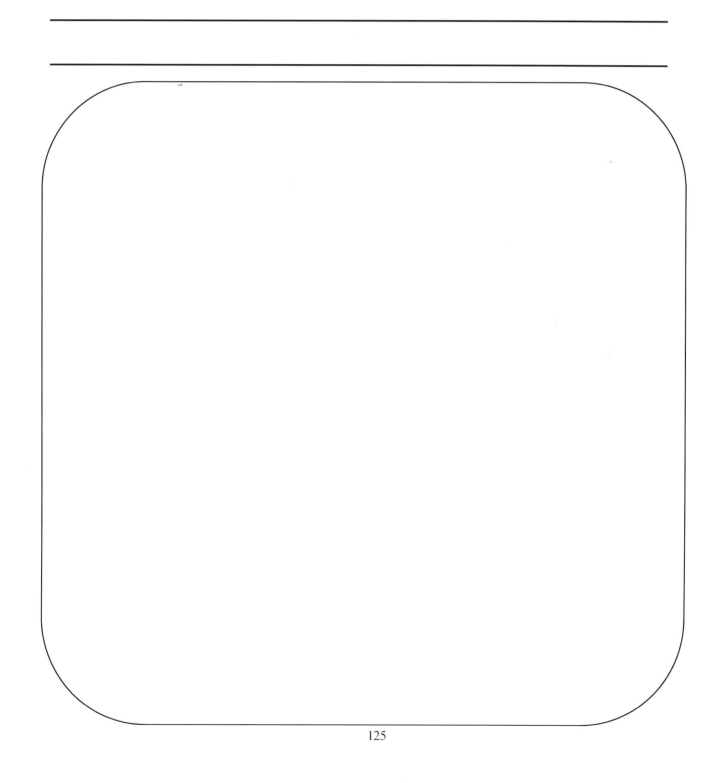

I. Verb Conjugation

Read, memorize, and copy the underlined words on the lines provided.

dormir (to sleep)

I sleep	yo <u>duermo</u>	_____
You sleep	tú <u>duermes</u>	_____
He/She sleeps	él/ella/Ud. <u>duerme</u>	_____
We sleep	nosotros/(as) <u>dormimos</u>	_____
You (all) sleep	vosotros/(as) <u>dormís</u>	_____
They sleep	Uds./ellos/ellas <u>duermen</u>	_____

II. Vocabulary

él......he   es......is
una rata......a rat   verde......green
duerme......he sleeps   bajo......under
la cama......the bed

III. Translation Practice

Read the sentence below and repeat in Spanish. Use the vocabulary above for help.

He sleeps under a green rat.

Model 3 Copy the Spanish sentence(s). Draw a picture.
Lesson 11
Él es una rata verde. Él duerme bajo la cama.

_____

_____

I. Verb Conjugation

Read, memorize, and copy the underlined words on the lines provided.

dormir (to sleep)

I sleep	yo <u>duermo</u>	_____
You sleep	tú <u>duermes</u>	_____
He/She sleeps	él/ella/Ud. <u>duerme</u>	_____
We sleep	nosotros/(as) <u>dormimos</u>	_____
You (all) sleep	vosotros/(as) <u>dormís</u>	_____
They sleep	Uds./ellos/ellas <u>duermen</u>	_____

II. Vocabulary

nosotros......we

en......in

bajo......under

dormimos......sleep

una cama......a bed

las estrellas......the stars

III. Translation Practice

Read the sentence below and repeat in Spanish. Use the vocabulary above for help.

We sleep under the stars.

Model 4 Copy the Spanish sentence(s). Draw a picture.

Lesson 11

Nosotros dormimos en una cama bajo las estrellas.

_____

_____

Verb Conjugation Review

Write the conjugation of the verb <u>dormir</u>. Use the previous page for help, if needed.

yo _____   nosotros/(as) _____

tú _____   vosotros/(as) _____

él/ella/Ud._____   Uds./ellos/ellas _____

Vocabulary Review

Translate the following words. Remember to add the appropriate article, <u>el</u>, <u>la</u>, <u>los</u>, or <u>las</u>. Use the vocabulary from the previous pages for help, if needed.

donkey   _____

white   _____

bumble bee   _____

flower   _____

bed   _____

stars   _____

under   _____

to sleep   _____

Model 5   Read these sentences.

Lesson 11

1. Yo soy un pequeño abejón. Yo duermo en una flor.

2. Tú eres un burro blanco. Tú duermes en una flor.

3. Él es una rata verde. El duerme bajo la cama.

4. Nosotros dormimos en una cama bajo las estrellas.

Translate one or more into English.

_____

_____

_____

_____

_____

_____

_____

_____

Lesson 11 Translations

Fun Spanish Sentences (Model Work)

1. Yo soy un pequeño abejón. Yo duermo en una flor.
2. Tú eres un burro blanco. Tú duermes en una flor.
3. Él es una rata verde. El duerme bajo la cama.
4. Nosotros dormimos en una cama bajo las estrellas.

1. I am a little bumblebee. I sleep in a flower.
2. You are a white donkey. You sleep in a flower.
3. He is a green rat. He sleeps under the bed.
4. We sleep in a bed under the stars.

Translation Practice (Days 1-4)

I am a little flower.	Yo soy una pequeña flor.
You are a white flower.	Tú eres una flor blanca.
He sleeps under a green rat.	Él duerme bajo una rata verde.
We sleep under the stars.	Nosotros dormimos bajo las estrellas.

Vocabulary Review (Day 5)

donkey	el burro
white	blanco
bumble bee	el abejón
flower	la flor
bed	la cama
stars	la estrellas
under	bajo
to sleep	dormir

LESSON 12

I. Verb Conjugation

Read, memorize, and copy the underlined words on the lines provided.

	querer (to want)	
I want	*yo* quiero	_____
You want	*tú* quieres	_____
He/She wants	*él/ella/Ud.* quiere	_____
We want	*nosotros/(as)* queremos	_____
You (all) want	*vosotros/(as)* quereis	_____
They want	*Uds./ellos/ellas* quieren	_____

II. Vocabulary

yo......I

una araña......a spider

comer......to eat

soy......I am

quiero......I want

(el) arroz......rice

III. Translation Practice

Read the sentence below and repeat in Spanish. Use the vocabulary above for help.

I want a spider.

Model / Copy the Spanish sentence(s). Draw a picture.
Lesson 12
Yo soy una araña. Yo quiero comer arroz.

_____

_____

I. Verb Conjugation

Read, memorize, and copy the underlined words on the lines provided.

querer (to want)

I want	*yo* <u>quiero</u>	_____
You want	*tú* <u>quieres</u>	_____
He/She wants	*él/ella/Ud.* <u>quiere</u>	_____
We want	*nosotros/(as)* <u>queremos</u>	_____
You (all) want	*vosotros/(as)* <u>quereis</u>	_____
They want	*Uds./ellos/ellas* <u>quieren</u>	_____

II. Vocabulary

tú......you

una araña......a spider

quieres......you want

eres......you are

también......also

comer......to eat

(los) espagueti......spaghetti

III. Translation Practice

Read the sentence below and repeat in Spanish. Use the vocabulary above for help.

You want spaghetti.

Model 2 Copy the Spanish sentence(s). Draw a picture.
Lesson 12
Tú eres una araña también. Tú quieres comer espagueti.

_____

_____

I. Verb Conjugation

Read, memorize, and copy the underlined words on the lines provided.

querer (to want)

I want	*yo* <u>quiero</u>	_____
You want	*tú* <u>quieres</u>	_____
He/She wants	*él/ella/Ud.* <u>quiere</u>	_____
We want	*nosotros/(as)* <u>queremos</u>	_____
You (all) want	*vosotros/(as)* <u>quereis</u>	_____
They want	*Uds./ellos/ellas* <u>quieren</u>	_____

II. Vocabulary

él…..he

una lagartija…..a lizard

comer…..to eat

es…..is

quiere…..he wants

(la) torta…..cake

III. Translation Practice

Read the sentence below and repeat in Spanish. Use the vocabulary above for help.

He wants a lizard.

Model 3 Copy the Spanish sentence(s). Draw a picture.
Lesson 12
Él es una lagartija. Él quiere comer torta.

_____

_____

I. Verb Conjugation

Read, memorize, and copy the underlined words on the lines provided.

	querer (to want)	
I want	*yo* <u>quiero</u>	_____
You want	*tú* <u>quieres</u>	_____
He/She wants	*él/ella/Ud.* <u>quiere</u>	_____
We want	*nosotros/(as)* <u>queremos</u>	_____
You (all) want	*vosotros/(as)* <u>quereis</u>	_____
They want	*Uds./ellos/ellas* <u>quieren</u>	_____

II. Vocabulary

nosotros.....we

hambre.....hunger

comer.....to eat

también.....also

tenemos.....have

queremos.....we want

(los) vegetales.....vegetables

III. Translation Practice

Read the sentence below and repeat in Spanish. Use the vocabulary above for help.

We want vegetables too.

Model 4 Copy the Spanish sentence(s). Draw a picture.
Lesson 12
Nosotros tenemos hambre. Nosotros queremos comer vegetales también.

_____

_____

Verb Conjugation Review

Write the conjugation of the verb <u>querer</u>. Use the previous page for help, if needed.

yo _____   nosotros/(as) _____

tú _____   vosotros/(as) _____

él/ella/Ud. _____   Uds./ellos/ellas _____

Vocabulary Review

Translate the following words. Remember to add the appropriate article, <u>el</u>, <u>la</u>, <u>los</u>, or <u>las</u>. Use the vocabulary from the previous pages for help, if needed.

spider _____

rice _____

too _____

spaghetti _____

lizard _____

cake _____

hungry _____

vegetables _____

to eat _____

Model 5   *Read these sentences.*

Lesson 12

1. Yo soy una araña. Yo quiero comer arroz.
2. Tú eres una araña también. Tú quieres comer espagueti.
3. Él es una lagartija. Él quiere comer torta.
4. Nosotros tenemos hambre. Nosotros queremos comer vegetales también.

Translate one or more into English.

_____

_____

_____

_____

_____

_____

_____

_____

Lesson 12 Translations

Fun Spanish Sentences (Model Work)

1. Yo soy una araña. Yo quiero comer arroz.
2. Tú eres una araña también. Tú quieres comer espagueti.
3. Él es una lagartija. Él quiere comer torta.
4. Nosotros tenemos hambre. Nosotros queremos comer vegetales también.

1. I am a spider. I want to eat rice.
2. You are a spider too. You want to eat spaghetti.
3. He is a lizard. He wants to eat cake.
4. We are hungry. We want to eat vegetables too.

Translation Practice (Days 1-4)

I want a spider.	Yo quiero una araña.
You want spaghetti.	Tú quieres espagueti.
He wants a lizard.	Él quiere una lagartija.
We want vegetables too.	Nosotros queremos vegetales también.

Vocabulary Review (Day 5)

spider	la araña	
rice	el arroz	
too	también	
spaghetti	el espagueti	
lizard	la lagartija	
cake	la torta	cake is also used
hungry	hambre	
vegetables	vegetales	
to eat	comer	

LESSON 13

I. Verb Conjugation

Read, memorize, and copy the underlined words on the lines provided.

estar (to be)

English	Spanish	
I am	yo <u>estoy</u>	_____
You are	tú <u>estás</u>	_____
He/She is	él/ella/Ud. <u>está</u>	_____
We are	nosotros/(as) <u>estamos</u>	_____
You (all) are	vosotros/(as) <u>estais</u>	_____
They are	Uds./ellos/ellas <u>están</u>	_____

II. Vocabulary

el niño......the boy

  está......is

    en......in

grande......big

    pequeño......little

    sentado......sitting

  la cuchara......the spoon

III. Translation Practice

Read the sentence below and repeat in Spanish. Use the vocabulary above for help.

The boy is in the spoon.

Model 1 Copy the Spanish sentence(s). Draw a picture.
Lesson 13
El niño pequeño está sentado en la cuchara grande.

I. Verb Conjugation

Read, memorize, and copy the underlined words on the lines provided.

	estar (to be)	
I am	*yo* <u>estoy</u>	_____
You are	*tú* <u>estás</u>	_____
He/She is	*él/ella/Ud.* <u>está</u>	_____
We are	*nosotros/(as)* <u>estamos</u>	_____
You (all) are	*vosotros/(as)* <u>estais</u>	_____
They are	*Uds./ellos/ellas* <u>están</u>	_____

II. Vocabulary

la cuchara......the spoon

bajo......under

y......and

el mono......the monkey

está......it is

la mesa......the table

sobre......on

III. Translation Practice

Read the sentence below and repeat in Spanish. Use the vocabulary above for help.

The monkey is under the table.

Model 2 Copy the Spanish sentence(s). Draw a picture.
Lesson 13
La cuchara está bajo la mesa y sobre el mono.

_____

_____

I. Verb Conjugation

Read, memorize, and copy the underlined words on the lines provided.

estar (to be)

I am	*yo* <u>estoy</u>	_____
You are	*tú* <u>estás</u>	_____
He/She is	*él/ella/Ud.* <u>está</u>	_____
We are	*nosotros/(as)* <u>estamos</u>	_____
You (all) are	*vosotros/(as)* <u>estais</u>	_____
They are	*Uds./ellos/ellas* <u>están</u>	_____

II. Vocabulary

el hermano......the brother

parado......standing

la silla......the chair

está......he is

en......on

(parado for standing is not a literal translation)

III. Translation Practice

Read the sentence below and repeat in Spanish. Use the vocabulary above for help.

The brother is on the chair.

Model 3 Copy the Spanish sentence(s). Draw a picture.
Lesson 13
El hermano está parado en la silla.

_____

_____

I. Verb Conjugation

Read, memorize, and copy the underlined words on the lines provided.

estar (to be)

I am	*yo* <u>estoy</u>	_____
You are	*tú* <u>estás</u>	_____
He/She is	*él/ella/Ud.* <u>está</u>	_____
We are	*nosotros/(as)* <u>estamos</u>	_____
You (all) are	*vosotros/(as)* <u>estais</u>	_____
They are	*Uds./ellos/ellas* <u>están</u>	_____

II. Vocabulary

la silla......the chair
detrás de......behind
y......and
el tenedor......the fork

está......is
el refrigerador......refrigerador
sobre......on

III. Translation Practice

Read the sentence below and repeat in Spanish. Use the vocabulary above for help.

The fork is behind the refrigerator.

Model 4 Copy the Spanish sentence(s). Draw a picture.

Lesson 13

La silla está detrás del refrigerador y sobre el tenedor.

_____

_____

Verb Conjugation Review

Write the conjugation of the verb _estar_. Use the previous page for help, if needed.

yo _____   nosotros/(as) _____

tú _____   vosotros/(as) _____

él/ella/Ud. _____   Uds./ellos/ellas _____

Vocabulary Review

Translate the following words. Remember to add the appropriate article, _el_, _la_, _los_, or _las_. Use the vocabulary from the previous pages for help, if needed.

boy   _____

spoon   _____

table   _____

on   _____

sitting   _____

chair   _____

refrigerator   _____

fork   _____

standing   _____

Model 5   **Read these sentences.**

Lesson 13

1. El niño pequeño está sentado en la cuchara grande.
2. La cuchara está bajo la mesa y sobre el mono.
3. El hermano está parado en la silla.
4. La silla está detrás del refrigerador y sobre el tenedor.

Translate one or more into English.

_____

_____

_____

_____

_____

_____

_____

_____

Lesson 13 Translations

Fun Spanish Sentences (Model Work)

1. El niño pequeño está senta do en la cuchara grande.
2. La cuchara está bajo la mesa y sobre el mono.
3. El hermano está parado en la silla.
4. La silla está detrás del refrigerador y sobre el tenedor.

1. The little boy is sitting in the big spoon.
2. The spoon is under the table and on the monkey.
3. The brother is standing on the chair.
4. The chair is behind the refrigerator and on the fork.

Translation Practice (Days 1-4)

The boy is in the spoon.
The monkey is under the table.
The brother is on the chair.
The fork is behind the refrigerator.

El niño está en la cuchara.
El mono está bajo la mesa.
El hermano está en la silla.
El tenedor está detrás del refrigerador.

Vocabulary Review (Day 5)

boy	el niño
spoon	la cuchara
table	la mesa
on	sobre
sitting	sentado
chair	la silla
refrigerator	el refrigerador
fork	el tenedor
standing	parado

LESSON 14

I. Verb Conjugation

Read, memorize, and copy the underlined words on the lines provided.

estar (to be)

I am	*yo* <u>estoy</u>	_____
You are	*tú* <u>estás</u>	_____
He/She is	*él/ella/Ud.* <u>está</u>	_____
We are	*nosotros/(as)* <u>estamos</u>	_____
You (all) are	*vosotros/(as)* <u>estais</u>	_____
They are	*Uds./ellos/ellas* <u>están</u>	_____

II. Vocabulary

el libro......the book   grande......big

está......it is   sobre......on

el sándwich......the sandwich

III. Translation Practice

Read the sentence below and repeat in Spanish. Use the vocabulary above for help.

The book is on the sandwich.

Model 1 Copy the Spanish sentence(s). Draw a picture.
Lesson 14
El libro grande está sobre el sándwich.

I. Verb Conjugation

Read, memorize, and copy the underlined words on the lines provided.

estar (to be)

I am	yo <u>estoy</u>	_____
You are	tú <u>estás</u>	_____
He/She is	él/ella/Ud. <u>está</u>	_____
We are	nosotros/(as) <u>estamos</u>	_____
You (all) are	vosotros/(as) <u>estais</u>	_____
They are	Uds./ellos/ellas <u>están</u>	_____

II. Vocabulary

el perro.......the dog
está.......he is
en.......on

gordo.......fat
parado.......standing
el plato.......the plate

(parado for standing is not a literal translation)

III. Translation Practice

Read the sentence below and repeat in Spanish. Use the vocabulary above for help.

The dog is on the plate.

Model 2 Copy the Spanish sentence(s). Draw a picture.
Lesson 14
El perro gordo está parado sobre el plato.

_____

_____

I. Verb Conjugation

Read, memorize, and copy the underlined words on the lines provided.

estar (to be)

I am	*yo* <u>estoy</u>	_____
You are	*tú* <u>estás</u>	_____
He/She is	*él/ella/Ud.* <u>está</u>	_____
We are	*nosotros/(as)* <u>estamos</u>	_____
You (all) are	*vosotros/(as)* <u>estais</u>	_____
They are	*Uds./ellos/ellas* <u>están</u>	_____

II. Vocabulary

el pato......the duck   rojo......red

está......he is   en......in

la taza......the cup   grande......big

III. Translation Practice

Read the sentence below and repeat in Spanish. Use the vocabulary above for help.

The duck is in the cup.

Model 3 Copy the Spanish sentence(s). Draw a picture.

Lesson 14

El pato rojo está en la taza grande.

_____

_____

I. Verb Conjugation

Read, memorize, and copy the underlined words on the lines provided.

estar (to be)

I am	yo <u>estoy</u>	_____
You are	tú <u>estás</u>	_____
He/She is	él/ella/Ud. <u>está</u>	_____
We are	nosotros/(as) <u>estamos</u>	_____
You (all) are	vosotros/(as) <u>estais</u>	_____
They are	Uds./ellos/ellas <u>están</u>	_____

II. Vocabulary

el pato......the duck

está......he is

agua......water

el inodoro......the toilet

rojo......red

bebiendo......drinking

de......from

(beber......drink)

del is a contraction of de and el

III. Translation Practice

Read the sentence below and repeat in Spanish. Use the vocabulary above for help.

The duck is in the toilet.   (en......in)

164

Model 4 Copy the Spanish sentence(s). Draw a picture.
Lesson 14
El pato rojo está bebiendo agua del inodoro.

_____

_____

Verb Conjugation Review

Write the conjugation of the verb <u>estar</u>. Use the previous page for help, if needed.

yo _____   nosotros/(as) _____

tú _____   vosotros/(as) _____

él/ella/Ud. _____   Uds./ellos/ellas _____

Vocabulary Review

Translate the following words. Remember to add the appropriate article, <u>el</u>, <u>la</u>, <u>los</u>, or <u>las</u>. Use the vocabulary from the previous pages for help, if needed.

fat   _____

plate   _____

duck   _____

book   _____

sandwich   _____

cup   _____

drinking   _____

water   _____

toilet   _____

Model 5   *Read these sentences.*

Lesson 14

1. El libro grande está sobre el sándwich.
2. El perro gordo está parado sobre el plato.
3. El pato rojo está en la taza grande.
4. El pato rojo está bebiendo agua del inodoro.

Translate one or more into English.

_____

_____

_____

_____

_____

_____

_____

_____

_____

Lesson 14 Translations

Fun Spanish Sentences (Model Work)

1. El libro grande está sobre el sándwich.
2. El perro gordo está parado sobre el plato.
3. El pato rojo está en la taza grande.
4. El pato rojo está bebiendo agua del inodoro.

1. The big book is on the sandwich.
2. The fat dog is standing on the plate.
3. The red duck is in the big cup.
4. The red duck is drinking water from the toilet.

Translation Practice (Days 1-4)

The book is on the sandwich.	El libro está sobre el sándwich.
The dog is on the plate.	El perro está sobre el plato.
The duck is in the cup.	El pato está en la taza.
The duck is in the toilet.	El pato está en el inodoro.

Vocabulary Review (Day 5)

fat	gordo
plate	el plato
duck	el pato
book	el libro
sandwich	el sándwich
cup	la taza
drinking	bebiendo
water	el agua
toilet	el inodoro

LESSON 15

I. Verb Conjugation

Read, memorize, and copy the underlined words on the lines provided.

ser (to be)

I am	*yo* <u>soy</u>	_____
You are	*tú* <u>eres</u>	_____
He/She is	*él/ella/Ud.* <u>es</u>	_____
We are	*nosotros/(as)* <u>somos</u>	_____
You (all)	*vosotros/(as)* <u>sois</u>	_____
They are	*Uds./ellos/ellas* <u>son</u>	_____

II. Vocabulary

el elefante......the elephant   es......is

    negro......black   pone......puts on

  las botas......the boots   se......himself

"se"—a reflexive form of the verb meaning himself, herself, or themselves

III. Translation Practice

Read the sentence below and repeat in Spanish. Use the vocabulary above for help.

The boots are black.

Model 1 Copy the Spanish sentence(s). Draw a picture.
Lesson 15

El elefante es negro. El elefante se pone las botas.

_____

_____

I. Verb Conjugation

Read, memorize, and copy the underlined words on the lines provided.

ser (to be)

I am	*yo* <u>soy</u>	_____
You are	*tú* <u>eres</u>	_____
He/She is	*él/ella/Ud.* <u>es</u>	_____
We are	*nosotros/(as)* <u>somos</u>	_____
You (all)	*vosotros/(as)* <u>sois</u>	_____
They are	*Uds./ellos/ellas* <u>son</u>	_____

II. Vocabulary

la serpiente......the snake   es......is

blanca......white   y......and

negra......black   pone......puts on

se......himself   un calcetín......one sock

"se"—a reflexive form of the verb meaning himself, herself, or themselves

---

III. Translation Practice

Read the sentence below and repeat in Spanish. Use the vocabulary above for help.

The sock is black and white.

Model 2 Copy the Spanish sentence(s). Draw a picture.
Lesson 15

La serpiente es negra y blanca. La serpiente se pone un calcetín.

_____

_____

I. Verb Conjugation

Read, memorize, and copy the underlined words on the lines provided.

ser (to be)

I am	yo **soy**	_____
You are	tú **eres**	_____
He/She is	él/ella/Ud. **es**	_____
We are	nosotros/(as) **somos**	_____
You (all)	vosotros/(as) **sois**	_____
They are	Uds./ellos/ellas **son**	_____

II. Vocabulary

la rata......the rat

azul......blue

seis......six

azules......blue

es......is

pone......puts on

(los) calcetines......socks

"se"—a reflexive form of the verb meaning himself, herself, or themselves

---

III. Translation Practice

Read the sentence below and repeat in Spanish. Use the vocabulary above for help.

The socks are blue.   (Use the verb conjugation for help.)

Model 3 Copy the Spanish sentence(s). Draw a picture.
Lesson 15

La rata es azul. La rata se pone seis
calcetines azules.

_____

_____

I. Verb Conjugation

Read, memorize, and copy the underlined words on the lines provided.

	ser (to be)	
I am	yo **soy**	_____
You are	tú **eres**	_____
He/She is	él/ella/Ud. **es**	_____
We are	nosotros/(as) **somos**	_____
You (all)	vosotros/(as) **sois**	_____
They are	Uds./ellos/ellas **son**	_____

II. Vocabulary

ellos......they

(los) vestidos......dresses

y......and

ponen......put on

rojos......red

(los) sombreros......hats

"se"—a reflexive form of the verb meaning himself, herself, or themselves

III. Translation Practice

Read the sentence below and repeat in Spanish. Use the vocabulary above for help.

They put on hats.   (Use "se".)

Model 4 Copy the Spanish sentence(s). Draw a picture.

Lesson 15

Ellos se ponen vestidos rojos y sombreros rojos.

_____

_____

Verb Conjugation Review

Write the conjugation of the verb _ser_. Use the previous page for help, if needed.

yo _____   nosotros/(as) _____

tú _____   vosotros/(as) _____

él/ella/Ud. _____   Uds./ellos/ellas _____

Vocabulary Review

Translate the following words. Remember to add the appropriate article, _el_, _la_, _los_, or _las_. Use the vocabulary from the previous pages for help, if needed.

boots   _____

white   _____

snake   _____

sock   _____

socks   _____

rat   _____

six   _____

dress   _____

hat   _____

Model 5   *Read these sentences.*

Lesson 15

1. El elefante es negro. El elefante se pone las botas.

2. La serpiente es negra y blanca. La serpiente se pone un calcetín.

3. La rata es azul. La rata se pone seis calcetines azules.

4. Ellos se ponen vestidos rojos y sombreros rojos.

Translate one or more into English.

_____

_____

_____

_____

_____

_____

_____

_____

Lesson 15 Translations

Fun Spanish Sentences (Model Work)

1. El elefante es negro. El elefante se pone las botas.
2. La serpiente es negra y blanca. La serpiente se pone un calcetín.
3. La rata es azul. La rata se pone seis calcetines azules.
4. Ellos se ponen vestidos rojos y sombreros rojos.

1. The elephant is black. The elephant puts on the boots.
2. The snake is black and white. The snake puts on a sock.
3. The rat is blue. The rat puts on six blue socks.
4. They put on red dresses and red hats.

Translation Practice (Days 1-4)

The boots are black.	Las botas son negras.
The sock is black and white.	El calcetín es blanco y negro.
The sock is blue.	Los calcetines son azules.
They put on hats.	Ellos se ponen sombreros.

Vocabulary Review (Day 5)

boots	la bota
white	blanco
snake	la serpiente
sock	el calcetín
socks	los calcetines
rat	la rata
six	seis
dress	el vestido
hat	el sombrero
to put	poner

LESSON 16

I. Verb Conjugation

Read, memorize, and copy the underlined words on the lines provided.

querer (to want)

I want	*yo* <u>quiero</u>	_____
You want	*tú* <u>quieres</u>	_____
He/She wants	*él/ella/Ud.* <u>quiere</u>	_____
We want	*nosotros/(as)* <u>queremos</u>	_____
You (all) want	*vosotros/(as)* <u>quereis</u>	_____
They want	*Uds./ellos/ellas* <u>quieren</u>	_____

II. Vocabulary

yo......I

un niño......a boy

muy......very

con......with

pequeños......little

soy......I am

morado......purple

alto......tall

(los) pies......feet

III. Translation Practice

Read the sentence below and repeat in Spanish. Use the vocabulary above for help.

I am a tall boy.

Model 1 Copy the Spanish sentence(s). Draw a picture.
Lesson 16
Yo soy un niño morado. Yo soy muy alto con
pies pequeños.

_____

_____

I. Verb Conjugation

Read, memorize, and copy the underlined words on the lines provided.

querer (to want)

I want	*yo* <u>quiero</u>	_____
You want	*tú* <u>quieres</u>	_____
He/She wants	*él/ella/Ud.* <u>quiere</u>	_____
We want	*nosotros/(as)* <u>queremos</u>	_____
You (all) want	*vosotros/(as)* <u>quereis</u>	_____
They want	*Uds./ellos/ellas* <u>quieren</u>	_____

II. Vocabulary

ella......she
una niña......a girl
muy......very
con......with
grandes......big

es......is
azul......blue
baja......short
(las) manos......hands

III. Translation Practice

Read the sentence below and repeat in Spanish. Use the vocabulary above for help.

She is a short girl.

Model 2 Copy the Spanish sentence(s). Draw a picture.
Lesson 16
Ella es una niña azul. Ella es muy baja con manos grandes.

_____

_____

I. Verb Conjugation

Read, memorize, and copy the underlined words on the lines provided.

	querer (to want)	
I want	*yo* quiero	_____
You want	*tú* quieres	_____
He/She wants	*él/ella/Ud.* quiere	_____
We want	*nosotros/(as)* queremos	_____
You (all) want	*vosotros/(as)* quereis	_____
They want	*Uds./ellos/ellas* quieren	_____

II. Vocabulary

mi......my

tiene.....has

rosados.....pink

y.....and

(el) padre......father

(los) ojos......eyes

grandes.....big

(el) pelo......hair

verde.....green

III. Translation Practice

Read the sentence below and repeat in Spanish. Use the vocabulary above for help.

My father has green eyes.

Model 3 Copy the Spanish sentence(s). Draw a picture.
Lesson 16
Mi padre tiene ojos grandes rosados y pelo verde.

_____

_____

I. Verb Conjugation

Read, memorize, and copy the underlined words on the lines provided.

querer (to want)

I want	*yo* quiero	_____
You want	*tú* quieres	_____
He/She wants	*él/ella/Ud.* quiere	_____
We want	*nosotros/(as)* queremos	_____
You (all) want	*vosotros/(as)* quereis	_____
They want	*Uds./ellos/ellas* quieren	_____

II. Vocabulary

su......her   (la) madre......mother

tiene......has   una nariz......a nose

larga......long   y......and

una boca......mouth   pequeña......little

III. Translation Practice

Read the sentence below and repeat in Spanish. Use the vocabulary above for help.

Her mother has a small nose.

Model 4 Copy the Spanish sentence(s). Draw a picture.
Lesson 16
Su madre tiene una nariz larga y una boca
pequeña.

_____

_____

Verb Conjugation Review

Write the conjugation of the verb <u>querer</u>. Use the previous page for help, if needed.

yo _____   nosotros/(as) _____

tú _____   vosotros/(as) _____

él/ella/Ud. _____   Uds./ellos/ellas _____

Vocabulary Review

Translate the following words. Remember to add the appropriate article, <u>el</u>, <u>la</u>, <u>los</u>, or <u>las</u>. Use the vocabulary from the previous pages for help, if needed.

purple   _____

tall   _____

feet   _____

girl   _____

hands   _____

father   _____

mother   _____

eyes   _____

nose   _____

mouth   _____

short   _____

Model 5   *Read these sentences.*

Lesson 16

1. Yo soy un niño morado. Yo soy muy alto con piés pequeños.

2. Ella es una niña azul. Ella es muy baja con manos grandes.

3. Mi padre tiene ojos grandes rosados y pelo verde.

4. Su madre tiene una nariz larga y una boca pequeña.

Translate one or more into English.

_____

_____

_____

_____

_____

_____

_____

_____

Lesson 16 Translations

Fun Spanish Sentences (Model Work)

1. Yo soy un niño morado. Yo soy muy alto con pies pequeños.
2. Ella es una niña azul. Ella es muy baja con manos grandes.
3. Mi padre tiene ojos grandes rosados y pelo verde.
4. Su madre tiene una nariz larga y una boca pequeña.

1. I am a purple boy. I am very tall with little feet.
2. She is a blue girl. She is very short with big hands.
3. My father has big pink eyes and green hair.
4. Her mother has a long nose and a small mouth.

Translation Practice (Days 1-4)

I am a tall boy.	Yo soy un niño alto.
She is short girl.	Ella es una niña baja.
My father has green eyes.	Mi padre tiene ojos verdes.
Her mother has a small nose.	Su madre tiene una nariz pequeña.

Vocabulary Review (Day 5)

purple	morada
tall	alto
feet	los pies
girl	la niña
hands	las manos
father	el padre
mother	la madre
eyes	los ojos
nose	la nariz
mouth	la boca
short	bajo/baja

LESSON 17

I. Verb Conjugation

Read, memorize, and copy the underlined words on the lines provided.

tener (to have)

I have	*yo* <u>tengo</u>	_____
You have	*tú* <u>tienes</u>	_____
He/She has	*él/ella/Ud.* <u>tiene</u>	_____
We have	*nosotros/(as)* <u>tenemos</u>	_____
You (all) have	*vosotros/(as)* <u>teneis</u>	_____
They have	*Uds./ellos/ellas* <u>tienen</u>	_____

II. Vocabulary

la niña......the girl

(los) pantalones......pants

su(s)......her

(las) piernas......legs

pone......put

sobre......on

(la) cabeza......head

III. Translation Practice

Read the sentence below and repeat in Spanish. Use the vocabulary above for help.

The girl puts pants on her legs.

Model / Copy the Spanish sentence(s). Draw a picture.

Lesson 17

La niña pone pantalones sobre su cabeza.

_____

_____

I. Verb Conjugation

Read, memorize, and copy the underlined words on the lines provided.

tener (to have)

I have	yo <u>tengo</u>	_____
You have	tú <u>tienes</u>	_____
He/She has	él/ella/Ud. <u>tiene</u>	_____
We have	nosotros/(as) <u>tenemos</u>	_____
You (all) have	vosotros/(as) <u>teneis</u>	_____
They have	Uds./ellos/ellas <u>tienen</u>	_____

II. Vocabulary

tú......you

zapatos......shoes

tus......your

los pies......feet

pones......put

sobre......on

orejas......ears

III. Translation Practice

Read the sentence below and repeat in Spanish. Use the vocabulary above for help.

You put shoes on your feet.

Model 2 Copy the Spanish sentence(s). Draw a picture.
Lesson 17
Tú pones zapatos sobre tus orejas.

_____

_____

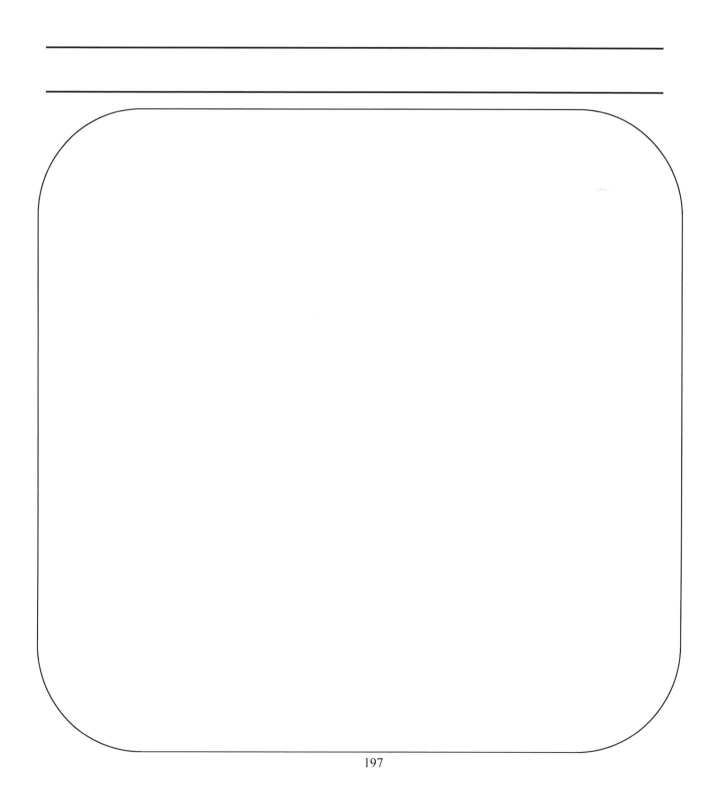

I. Verb Conjugation

Read, memorize, and copy the underlined words on the lines provided.

tener (to have)

I have	yo <u>tengo</u>	_____
You have	tú <u>tienes</u>	_____
He/She has	él/ella/Ud. <u>tiene</u>	_____
We have	nosotros/(as) <u>tenemos</u>	_____
You (all) have	vosotros/(as) <u>teneis</u>	_____
They have	Uds./ellos/ellas <u>tienen</u>	_____

II. Vocabulary

el niño......the boy

(la) camisas......shirts

sus......his

pone......put

en......on

(los) brazos......arms

III. Translation Practice

Read the sentence below and repeat in Spanish. Use the vocabulary above for help.

The boy puts on a shirt.

Model 3 Copy the Spanish sentence(s). Draw a picture.
Lesson 17
El niño pone camisas en sus brazos.

_____

_____

I. Verb Conjugation

Read, memorize, and copy the underlined words on the lines provided.

tener (to have)

I have	*yo* <u>tengo</u>	_____
You have	*tú* <u>tienes</u>	_____
He/She has	*él/ella/Ud.* <u>tiene</u>	_____
We have	*nosotros/(as)* <u>tenemos</u>	_____
You (all) have	*vosotros/(as)* <u>teneis</u>	_____
They have	*Uds./ellos/ellas* <u>tienen</u>	_____

II. Vocabulary

nosotros.....we

(los) calcetines.....socks

nuestras.....our

(los) pies.....feet

ponemos.....put

sobre.....on

(las) manos.....hands

III. Translation Practice

Read the sentence below and repeat in Spanish. Use the vocabulary above for help.

We put socks on our feet.

Model 4 Copy the Spanish sentence(s). Draw a picture.
Lesson 17
Nosotros ponemos calcetines sobre nuestras manos.

_____

_____

Verb Conjugation Review

Write the conjugation of the verb <u>tener</u>. Use the previous page for help, if needed.

yo _____   nosotros/(as) _____

tú _____   vosotros/(as) _____

él/ella/Ud. _____   Uds./ellos/ellas _____

Vocabulary Review

Translate the following words. Remember to add the appropriate article, <u>el</u>, <u>la</u>, <u>los</u>, or <u>las</u>. Use the vocabulary from the previous pages for help, if needed.

girl   _____

pants   _____

shoes   _____

ears   _____

boy   _____

shirt   _____

head   _____

on   _____

arms   _____

hands   _____

Model 5   *Read these sentences.*

Lesson 17

1. La niña pone pantalones sobre su cabeza.
2. Tú pones zapatos sobre tus orejas.
3. El niño pone camisas en sus brazos.
4. Nosotros ponemos calcetines sobre
nuestras manos.

Translate one or more into English.

_____

_____

_____

_____

_____

_____

_____

_____

Lesson 17 Translations

Fun Spanish Sentences (Model Work)

1. La niña pone pantalones sobre su cabeza.
2. Tú pones zapatos sobre tus orejas.
3. El niño pone camisas en sus brazos.
4. Nosotros ponemos calcetines sobre nuestras manos.

1. The girl puts pants on her head.
2. You put shoes over your ears.
3. The boy puts shirts on his arms.
4. We put socks on our hands.

Translation Practice (Days 1-4)

The girl puts pants on her legs.

La niña pone pantalones sobre sus piernas.

You put shoes on your feet.
Tú pones zapatos sobre tus pies.

The boy puts on a shirt.
El niño se pone una camisa.

We put socks on our feet.
Nosotros ponemos calcetines sobre nuestros pies.

Vocabulary Review (Day 5)

girl	la niña
pants	los pantalones
shoes	los zapatos
ears	las orejas
boy	el niño
shirt	la camisa
head	la cabeza
on	sobre
arms	los brazos
hands	las manos

32637612R00123

Made in the USA
San Bernardino, CA
12 April 2016